Bible Wisdom Devotions for Girls

Jean Fischer

Bible Wisdom Devotions for Girls

BARBOUR kidz
A Division of Barbour Publishing

YOU are the reason we do what we do here at Barbour Publishing. We promise that we will always use our God-given talents to produce content with you in mind—and that we will remain biblically faithful, no matter what.

Thank you for being the heart of our business.

ISBN 979-8-89151-265-8

Published by Barbour Publishing, Inc., 1810 Barbour Drive, Uhrichsville, Ohio 44683, www.barbourbooks.com

Our mission is to inspire the world with the life-changing message of the Bible.

Printed in China.

002806 0126 DS

INTRODUCTION

These devotions and prayers were created just for you, girl!

Take a few minutes each day to nourish your blossoming spirit with these inspiring and encouraging devotions, scriptures, and prayers that will draw you closer to God's heart and fill your soul with everlasting joy.

Touching on topics like choices, kindness, love, loyalty, honesty, and so much more, these just-right-sized readings will meet you right where you are in life. *Bible Wisdom Devotions for Girls* is a great way to help you grow in your faith!

"I will be a Father to you. You will be My. . .
daughters, says the All-powerful God."
2 CORINTHIANS 6:18 NLV

WHO *IS* THAT GIRL?

I will give thanks to You, for the greatness of the way I was made brings fear. Your works are great and my soul knows it very well.

PSALM 139:14 NLV

Look in the mirror. Who *is* that girl looking back at you? Why, she's a perfect creation, a work of art! God, the great Creator of everything—the same God who made the sun, the moon and stars, the towering mountains and the vast oceans—made you! When He looks at you, God sees His girl, His child, perfectly and wonderfully made. God didn't make you to be ordinary or random. Not at all! He made you with a specific purpose. God has your whole life planned, and His plan for you is perfect. You can't know yet everything God has waiting for you. Much of it is secret. He will reveal His plan to you little by little throughout your whole life. Your job right now is to trust that God's plan for you is good.

Dear God, help me to see myself as You see me. Help me to trust You every day of my life. Amen.

TRUE BEAUTY

Do not let your beauty come from the outside. It should not be the way you comb your hair or the wearing of gold or the wearing of fine clothes. Your beauty should come from the inside. It should come from the heart.

1 PETER 3:3–4 NLV

When you look at yourself in the mirror, do you hope to see a girl with perfectly styled hair? A girl wearing cool clothes on a perfect body? A girl with perfect skin? Perfect teeth? Perfect everything? True beauty has nothing to do with how you look on the outside. Instead, it comes from your heart. When God made you, He filled your heart with all the good stuff: things like love, kindness, generosity, forgiveness, thoughtfulness, caring, respectfulness, courage, strength, politeness, responsibility, and more. God filled your heart with everything that makes you—you! When you care more about what's inside your heart than your image in the mirror, then you will be pleased with yourself just as you are. And when you let others see what's inside your heart, your beauty will shine like the brightest star.

Dear God, remind me always that I'm beautiful both inside and out. Amen.

MAKE GOD YOUR EVERYTHING

God is in the center of her. She will not be moved.
God will help her when the morning comes.
PSALM 46:5 NLV

God sees you. He has the amazing ability to be everywhere all the time at the same time. God knows everything. There's nothing about you He doesn't know or see. That might make you feel a little uneasy. God isn't spying on you. He's not watching and waiting for you to do something wrong so He can punish you. God's plan is to guide you through your life. When you make Him your everything, when you make God the center of your universe, great things will happen. He will add His power and strength to all those good things He put inside your heart. God will make you strong enough to stand up to whatever trouble comes your way. When you make God your everything, you can count on Him to help you all day every day forever!

Dear God, I want You to be my everything. Teach me to put all my faith and trust in You. Be my guide every day. Amen.

WHAT IS SIN?

If you know what is right to do
but you do not do it, you sin.
JAMES 4:17 NLV

There's that word—*sin*. Maybe you know what it means, kind of. But what is sin really? A sin is anything a person does that God says isn't right. You learn what God says is right by reading the Bible. Your heart also helps you know the difference between right and wrong. There's a little voice inside your heart that says, *"Stop. Don't do that."* Some people call it their conscience. But that voice is really the Holy Spirit of God reminding you to make the right choice. No one is perfect. Everybody is guilty of sin. As hard as you try to please God, you will never be able to please Him 100 percent. What's awesome about God, though, is that when you sin He will always forgive you. Tell Him what you did, ask for His forgiveness, and He will erase that sin as if it never happened.

Dear God, I did something today that I know is wrong. I'm sorry. Please forgive me. Amen.

SAVED!

"Today in the town of David a Savior has been born to you; he is the Messiah, the Lord."
LUKE 2:11 NIV

From the beginning, when God created the first humans, people sinned. They kept trying to please God, and they failed. Sin separated people from God, and God didn't like that. He wanted everyone to be made right with Him, so He made a plan. He decided to send His Son, Jesus, into the world to save His people from sin. Jesus took all the world's sin on Himself, and He suffered all the punishment for the wrong things people did and would forever do. God said if people believed that Jesus had taken the punishment they deserved, they were promised life forever in heaven after they died. God makes that promise to you! If you believe that Jesus took the punishment for the wrong things you do and you ask Him to come into your heart, He will stay with you forever.

Dear Jesus, thank You for saving us from the sin that separates us from God. And thank You for promising us life forever with You in heaven. Amen.

ROLE MODEL

Do as God would do. Much-loved children want to do as their fathers do.
EPHESIANS 5:1 NLV

Is there someone you look up to as a role model, someone whom you respect and want to be like? It's okay to have people as role models, but the best role model of all is Jesus. He is just like God, His Father. So when you try to be more like Jesus, you are becoming more like God. You can read the story of Jesus' life in the Bible in the New Testament books Matthew, Mark, Luke, and John. As you read and learn about Jesus and model your behavior after His, you will be growing into the kind of girl God wants you to be. As you become more like Jesus, others will see Jesus in your actions and words. If they say, "I want to be more like her!" then you will have become *their* role model. (How cool is that!) How well do you know Jesus? Can you name some of His qualities? Things like forgiving, loving, caring. . .

Dear Jesus, I want to learn about You and become more like You. Amen.

THE GREATEST LAW

Jesus said to him, "'You must love the Lord your God with all your heart and with all your soul and with all your mind.' This is the first and greatest of the Laws."

MATTHEW 22:37–38 NLV

When someone asked Jesus which is the greatest of God's laws, He answered, "You must love the Lord your God with all your heart and with all your soul and with all your mind." How can you show God you love Him? By doing your best to follow His commands, reading the Bible and obeying its words, praying to God, trusting Him, and thanking Him for all the good things He does for you. And praising Him too, because He is the one and only God. Putting God first is the most important thing you can do. When you ask Him to lead you in everything from the tiniest actions and decisions to the biggest ones, you let loose His power in your life. God's power working through you is all you need to accomplish more than you can imagine.

Dear God, You have first place in my life. You come before anyone or anything else. Amen.

WHO IS MY NEIGHBOR?

"The second is like it, 'You must love your neighbor as you love yourself.'"
MATTHEW 22:39 NLV

It doesn't matter to God what people look like, whether they are a girl or boy, or even if they are young or old. God made everyone. We are all His children. And while He made each of us special and unique, we are alike because we have the same needs. Every one of us has hopes and dreams. We all worry about things, and sometimes we feel afraid. We always need friends to share in our good times and bad. Jesus said the second greatest of God's laws is "You must love your neighbor as you love yourself." This law tells us that God wants us to treat every- one with love and respect. He wants us to set our selfishness aside to be giving and to share with one another. Who is your neighbor? Everyone on earth is your neighbor, everyone near and far.

Dear God, please help me not to be selfish. Help me to remember that everyone has needs, just as I do. And help me to be giving. Amen.

A HEARTFELT CONNECTION

May the Lord lead your hearts
into the love of God.
2 THESSALONIANS 3:5 NLV

The Bible says that God is love. God created you because He loves you and He wants a loving relationship with you. God's love is different from human love. God doesn't love you because your good behavior pleases Him. He doesn't love you because you're cute, fun to be with, and lovable. God's love is unconditional. That means even if your behavior was the worst of the worst, and even if you wanted nothing to do with Him, God would still love you. God's love is absolutely perfect. He would do anything for you, even allow His Son to take the punishment for your sins so you can live with Him someday in heaven. God wants His heart and yours to be connected in love. That's one reason He gave us Jesus—to teach us about love so we can share it with others. Can you think of some ways to share God's love?

Dear God, thank You for loving me no matter what. Teach me what it means to love others the way You love them. Amen.

LOVE IS PATIENT

Be completely humble and gentle;
be patient, bearing with one another in love.
EPHESIANS 4:2 NIV

Grown-ups can be so poky! Maybe you wanted to go to a friend's house, but Mom and Dad were too busy to take you. They told you to wait awhile. Did you complain, or did you wait patiently? Imagine you are in your room listening to music and reading. Your younger sibling keeps hanging around bothering you. Would you say, "Stop that" or "Go away"? Think about it: How patient are you? The Bible says love is patient. Patience is about waiting. It's also remembering that your annoying little sister or brother looks up to you and wants to spend time with you. Being patient isn't easy. But patience is one way to show others you love them. God is patient with you all the time. Every day you do things that displease Him, but, always, God forgives you, and He waits patiently while you try to do better next time.

Dear God, please help me to be more patient. Remind me that being patient shows others that I love them. Amen.

PATIENCE TAKES PRACTICE

Learn from the farmer. He waits for the good fruit from the earth until the early and late rains come.

JAMES 5:7 NLV

When you want something badly, it comes with a feeling that you want it right away. But most of the time you have to wait. Waiting patiently is something you learn. If you practice waiting with a good attitude, your patience will grow. James 5:7 says that farmers wait a long time for their seeds to become plants that produce good food. Farmers have faith that, in time, the seeds they plant will provide the crops they hope for. Wouldn't it be silly for a farmer to plant seeds and expect fully grown plants to pop out of the ground? When you ask God for something, He wants you to have faith, like a farmer, and wait for Him to answer your prayer. Practice waiting patiently. God loves you. Trust that He's working on a plan to give you something good.

Dear God, I know You hear me when I ask You for something. I trust You to answer my prayers, and I will practice waiting patiently for You to answer. Amen.

LOVE IS KIND

"You must have loving-kindness just as your Father has loving-kindness."

LUKE 6:36 NLV

Jesus said we should be kind to others the way God is kind toward us. Can you think of some ways God has been kind to you? Kindness is all about recognizing when someone is in need and then doing something to help. You can see people doing little acts of kindness all around you: people holding doors open for others, helping to carry groceries from the car to the house, pitching in with chores, feeding the birds, smiling, saying hello, complimenting one another. . . Kindness is about caring for others: comforting someone who is sad, sending a card to someone who is sick, checking on an elderly neighbor, sharing what you have. . . Kindness is also about including others: welcoming the new kid in class, teaching someone a new game, making new friends and inviting them to have fun with you. . . Kindness is another way of sharing God's love.

Dear God, open my eyes to the needs of others. Teach me to be kind and caring toward everyone I meet. Amen.

KINDNESS IS CONTAGIOUS

"Those who show loving-kindness are happy, because they will have loving-kindness shown to them."
MATTHEW 5:7 NLV

She has something contagious! Oh no, stay away from her! When you hear the word *contagious*, does it make you feel jittery? Does it make you want to run in the opposite direction? Let's give that word a new meaning, something positive. *Kindness is contagious.* Give it a try. Video chat with your grandparents and see their faces light up with smiles. Play with your dog and watch how his tail wags with delight. Read a book to your baby sister and notice how she snuggles up close to you, hanging on your every word. Jesus said that those who show loving-kindness are happy because they will have loving-kindness shown to them. When you show kindness to someone and it makes them happy, it gives you a happy feeling too. The happier you feel as a result of your kindness, the more likely you are to continue being kind. Kindness is something you want to spread around.

Dear God, I need some ideas. What kind things can I do today that will make others feel happy? Amen.

Kindness Is My Responsibility

Each person must be responsible for himself.
Galatians 6:5 NCV

Kindness is about taking responsibility for your actions. It's saying to yourself at the start of each day, *Today I'm going to. . .*, and then sticking with your plan. You could start by telling yourself, *Today I'm going to be kind to everyone*. But that's not enough. You need to have some ideas of how you will spread your kindness around. Make a list: *Today I'm going to compliment someone for doing a good job. Today I'm going to do something helpful for my parents without being asked. I will smile and say hello today. I will notice if someone is struggling with something, and I'll help.* When you make a list and follow through, you will be growing the loving-kindness God has already put inside your heart. The Bible says, "Each person must be responsible for himself." Today and every day you are responsible for sharing God's loving-kindness with others.

Dear God, when You created me,
You put Your loving-kindness in my heart
so I can share it with others. It's my
responsibility. Help me to do it well. Amen.

LOVE IS NEVER SELFISH

Nothing should be done because of pride or thinking about yourself. Think of other people as more important than yourself.

PHILIPPIANS 2:3 NLV

You are a girl who cares about others! You are a girl who sees when people are in trouble, and you jump right in to help. You are always thinking about others and what they need. Good for you! But not everyone is unselfish like you are. Can you think of examples of selfishness? Selfishness is always wanting stuff for yourself instead of giving to others. It is thinking about what you want and need without noticing the wants and needs of those around you. Selfishness is not seeing or caring when someone is feeling sad, lonely, discouraged, or afraid. It is not appreciating what you have and always wanting more. By acting *unselfishly*, the way you do, you are setting a good example for others. By being unselfish, you are helping to spread God's love around. Keep it up. Keep on being the kind, patient, caring girl you are.

Dear God, please guide us all to unselfish love and care for each other. Amen.

MORE LIKE JESUS

I want to please everyone in all that I do. I am not thinking of myself. I want to do what is best for them so they may be saved from the punishment of sin.
1 CORINTHIANS 10:33 NLV

Whatever Jesus did, He thought about what was best for others. He wanted everyone to be saved from facing any punishment for the sinful things they did. Jesus was never selfish. When people asked for His time, He gave it willingly. Jesus provided food when people were hungry. He healed them when they were sick. Even when He was tired, Jesus kept going, putting the needs of others before His own. The best thing you can do for yourself and others is to try your hardest to be more like Jesus. Do everything with the goal of pleasing God. If someone asks for help, give it willingly. If someone needs food, clothes, or something else, be ready to share what you have. God's love for you is never-ending. He is always thinking about and caring for you. It pleases Him to see you loving and caring about others.

Dear Jesus, teach me to be more like You. Amen.

LOVE IS NEVER SNOOTY

Love does not put itself up as being important. Love has no pride.
1 CORINTHIANS 13:4 NLV

"Snooty" describes someone who thinks she is too good for everyone and everything. She looks down at everyone and thinks she's better. It's hard for snooty people to love others just as much as it's hard for others to love those who are snooty. True love means loving others just because we are all created by the same God. He didn't make any one of us to be the prettiest, richest, or most popular. God gives each of us the ability to choose how we will live and how we will love. We can follow God's example and love each other equally, or we can choose not to follow God and choose to love some people and not others. Snootiness often leads to hurt feelings. No one likes being made to feel they are not good enough. Love is all about making people feel important and cared for. What can you do today to make others feel good about themselves and loved?

Dear God, remind me to treat everyone the same. No one is better than another. Amen.

HEY, LOOK AT ME!

Live and work without pride. Be gentle and kind.
Do not be hard on others. Let love keep you from doing that.
EPHESIANS 4:2 NLV

Yay! Good for you! You worked hard and accomplished something great. Your heart is filled with happiness. You feel even better when others celebrate what you've done. It's great to feel good about reaching your goals. But it's important to remember who helped you get there. Without God you wouldn't have the talents or skills that led to your big win. It's okay to take pride in what you do, but too much pride is like closing the door on God and not inviting Him to your celebration. Maybe you've seen athletes or actors accept awards and then thank God for His help. That's a good example for you to follow. Thank God for helping you. Then take it one step further. Help others to reach their goals. Be gentle and kind and happy for others when they win. That's a loving thing to do.

Dear God, thank You for helping me reach my goal. I couldn't have done it without You. Amen.

GETTING TO KNOW YOU

Love never thinks of itself.
1 CORINTHIANS 13:5 NLV

Let's see if you can answer these questions: What is each of your siblings' favorite thing to do? What is your grandmother's best childhood memory? What does your best friend worry about? Do you know someone who could use a little help? You learn about people by wanting to get to know them and asking questions. When a new kid comes to your school, a simple question like "Where did you go to school before?" gets a conversation going, and it might even begin a new friendship. The Bible says, "Love never thinks of itself." If you're all wrapped up in you, then it's hard to notice others and care about getting to know them. Asking questions like "What would you like to do today?" or "Do you need a little help with that?" or "Is something bothering you?" shows that you care. Give it a try today. Turn your thoughts toward others. See if you can get to know your family members and friends even better.

Dear God, teach me to care even more for others by getting to know them well. Amen.

LOVE IS SERVING OTHERS

Everything we do shows we are God's servants.
2 CORINTHIANS 6:4 NLV

Jesus always focused His thoughts on others. He was a servant to their needs. You can be more like Jesus and share His love with others by serving them. That means keeping your eyes open to their needs and taking action to help. God gave you a caring heart and things you are good at. When you combine caring with what you do well, you can make a difference in your community. It doesn't need to be something big. If you are good at art, you could make cards for kids in the hospital. If you enjoy singing, you could encourage your church's youth group to do a sing-along at a nursing home. Are you good at a subject in school? You could guide those who need a little help. Use your imagination. Be creative. When you become God's servant, His love will grow even bigger inside your heart. The more love you have, the more love you'll have to give to others.

Dear God, please give me some ideas of how I can serve others. Amen.

THE RIGHT PATH

Love does not do the wrong thing.
1 CORINTHIANS 13:5 NLV

If a friend wanted you to do something you know is wrong, would you do it, or would you be brave enough to say no? Saying no to sin isn't always easy. Some kids worry that if they don't join in, their friends won't like them. But think about this: Is it more important what God thinks or what your friends think? God loves you. He wants you to make wise choices and do what's good and right. Choosing the right path pleases God and shows that you love Him. Taking the right path makes you a leader instead of a follower. When you do what's right, you set a good example for others. You show them the difference between right and wrong, and that's a loving thing to do. Can you think of a time when a friend asked you to do something wrong and you said no? How did it make you feel?

Dear God, lead me to know the difference between right and wrong and to never be afraid to choose what is right. Amen.

A SHORT FUSE

Love does not get angry.
1 CORINTHIANS 13:5 NLV

Do you know what a pyrotechnician is? It's the person responsible for handling fireworks at holiday and other celebrations. They have an important job, because if not handled right, those fireworks could misfire and hurt people. Imagine if a firework's fuse, the part that's lit on fire, was too short. The pyrotechnician wouldn't have enough time to get out of the way before the firework exploded. A short fuse is dangerous. You might compare how you handle anger to the way a pyrotechnician works. Maybe your anger is like a short fuse that's ready to blow. When it pops, you explode with words and actions that can be hurtful to others. The Bible reminds us that love doesn't get angry. Love means learning to control what you say and do so you don't hurt those around you. It's important to think not only about how you feel but also about how your feelings might affect others. How do you measure up? Does your anger have a short fuse?

Dear God, please teach me to control
my anger and to treat others
with loving-kindness. Amen.

GET OVER IT!

If you are angry, do not let it become sin.
Get over your anger before the day is finished.
EPHESIANS 4:26 NLV

Feeling angry is normal. But anger that lasts isn't. Anger that causes you to do things like yell, throw things, and slam doors is never good. There are ways to calm down that anger. First, give yourself a time-out. Go someplace quiet where you can take a few deep breaths, slow down, and get yourself under control. Then talk with someone you trust, like a parent, teacher, or other older friend. Tell them what's bothering you. They might have some advice for how you can solve your problem. Sometimes taking a walk or doing something you enjoy can help angry feelings settle. Everyone gets angry sometimes. Notice what others do with their angry feelings. Model your behavior after those who handle anger well. Most of all, talk with God when you're angry. Give that angry feeling to Him and ask Him to replace it with love.

Dear God, I'm feeling angry. Please help me to calm down. I don't want to say or do anything that will make things worse. Thank You, God. Amen.

LOVE DOESN'T KEEP SCORE

[Love] keeps no record of wrongs.
1 CORINTHIANS 13:5 NIV

Maybe your sister likes to borrow your things. The problem is she doesn't always ask for your permission. You see her wearing one of your favorite T-shirts, and of course she didn't ask. So you say, "How many times have I told you not to do that?" Wait. Listen to your words. You've been keeping score. The Bible says that love keeps no record of wrongs. So what might you do instead? When neither of you is upset or angry, you could have a quiet talk with your sister. Explain why it upsets you that she doesn't ask first. Then make a plan to solve the problem. You might agree on certain things that require asking and others that don't. Love means not counting up how many times a person does something wrong. Your sister might mess up and forget again to ask for permission. Forgive her. Keep working at finding a loving way to get her to respect your things.

Dear God, guide me to be patient
when people mess up again and again.
I do that sometimes too. Amen.

HOW MANY TIMES?

Jesus said to him, "I tell you, not seven times but seventy times seven!"
MATTHEW 18:22 NLV

Jesus' disciple Peter came to Jesus and asked, "Lord, how many times may my brother sin against me and I forgive him, up to seven times?" (Matthew 18:21 NLV). Jesus' answer likely surprised Peter. He said, "I tell you, not seven times but seventy times seven!" If you did the math, you know that's 490 times! Jesus used that big number as an example to remind us we should always forgive those who sin against us. Why should we be that forgiving? Because God always forgives us when we sin. Always. And He expects us to do our best to be like Him. To be that forgiving takes practice. Forgiveness doesn't immediately erase the hurt or anger we feel when someone treats us badly. But forgiveness is the starting point for those bad feelings to heal. When you need to forgive someone, ask Jesus to help you. He knows better than anyone what it means to forgive.

Dear Jesus, someone hurt my feelings badly.
I want to forgive that person,
but it's hard. Will You help me? Amen.

FATHER, FORGIVE THEM

Then Jesus said, "Father, forgive them.
They do not know what they are doing."
LUKE 23:34 NLV

Jesus suffered many things during His last days here on earth. One of His disciples, His friend Judas, turned Jesus over to those who wanted to kill Him. When Jesus was arrested, all His disciples left Him and ran away. Jesus was accused of many things, but He had done nothing wrong. He was spit on, made fun of, whipped, and slapped. Then those in charge made Jesus carry a heavy wooden cross to a nearby hill. There they nailed His hands and feet to the cross, set the cross upright, and left Jesus to die. What did Jesus say when they hung Him there? "Father, forgive them. They do not know what they are doing." Could you be that forgiving? When people hurt your feelings, think of Jesus. He understands what it means to forgive. When you need to forgive someone and forgiveness is hard, do what Jesus did. Ask God to forgive them.

Dear heavenly Father, [name of person] has hurt my feelings. I don't think [he/she] meant to hurt me. Please forgive [him/her]. Amen.

THE HONEST TRUTH

Love is not happy with sin. Love is happy with the truth.
1 CORINTHIANS 13:6 NLV

True or false? (1) Sydney is the capital of Australia. (2) Camels can store water in their humps. (3) A group of monkeys is called a herd. The answer to all three is "false." How well did you do? It's not always easy separating true from false. God loves the truth, and He wants us to seek out the truth in all things. You learn the truth by doing research and finding facts. When it comes to knowing the truth about what is right and what is wrong, the Bible is your best resource. God rules the universe, and He decides what is right and wrong. Every word of the Bible is true. You can always trust what God says. So if you are ever confused about whether something is right or wrong, search the Bible. It will always give you the honest truth. Can you name a few things you're unsure of? Make time this week to uncover the facts.

Dear God, remind me not to believe everything I hear but instead to seek the truth. Amen.

TELL THE TRUTH WITH LOVE

We are to hold to the truth with love in our hearts.
We are to grow up and be more like Christ.
EPHESIANS 4:15 NLV

One way to show love for God and others is to tell the truth. If you've done something wrong, it might be hard to admit it. But you know you should. If you see someone else do something wrong, it's good to tell the truth about that too. If a little voice inside tells you to lie, that's not God. He will always tell you to be truthful. Do you know how to tell someone what they did is wrong? Pray before you speak. Ask God to give you the right words. Saying things like "I saw what you did!" or "Shame on you" will just make the other person feel guiltier. Talk with the person in private. Tell the truth with love. Be gentle, kind, and caring. Let the other person know you love them and are just trying to be helpful. With love in your heart, telling the truth is easier.

Dear God, I promise I'll do my best to be truthful. Amen.

HEY EVIL, TAKE THAT!

Love is not happy with evil.
1 Corinthians 13:6 NIRV

The Bible says love isn't happy with evil. There are plenty of evil things in the world to be unhappy about, things like hunger and homelessness or storms and fires that damage possessions and the earth. You could make a longer list, but instead, how about doing something to turn evil into good? It's important to remember that God doesn't cause evil. He hates it. God is all about love. He wants us to stand up to evil. Can you think of ways to do that? If people are hungry, you can give them food. If some are homeless, you can help by donating clothing and other things they need. If a bad storm knocks down trees, you can help plant new ones. There are many good things a girl like you can do. So get busy and do your best to bring some love into the world. Then when you're all done, you can tell evil, "Take that!"

Dear God, I've decided that instead of thinking about what's evil in the world, I'm going to do something good! Amen.

GOD PROTECTS ME

[Love] always protects.
1 CORINTHIANS 13:7 NIV

You're the sort of girl who protects her younger sisters and brothers. If you see them running toward a busy street or about to do anything else that's dangerous, you rush in to stop them from getting hurt. You probably protect any pets you have too. If you take your dog for a walk, you make sure its collar is fastened and you hold tight to the leash. You're the kind of girl who wants everyone to be safe. Protecting someone is a very loving thing to do. God protects you because He loves you. God is with you everywhere you go. Nothing happens without Him knowing. If something bad happens, you might think God isn't with you. But He is! God will always keep you safe in your spirit, the place where He lives inside you. You don't have to be afraid, because God is always right there with you inside your heart. The closer you get to trusting Him, the safer you will feel, no matter what.

Dear God, thank You for staying with me inside my heart and for being my protector. Amen.

TRUST IN GOD

[Love] always trusts.
1 CORINTHIANS 13:7 NIV

God, the Creator of the universe, loves you. Do you believe that? The one who made everything and has power over everything loves you! God is trustworthy. God knows everything all the time. Everything He does is right. God doesn't change, and you can always trust in His Word. The first step to trusting God is to pray and give all your problems and troubles to Him. Ask for His help. You know that God hears you. Then practice being patient while remembering that God's timing is always perfect. While you're waiting, think about how God has blessed and taken care of you. It might help to write those things down. God will always provide for you exactly what you need when you need it. If you find yourself not trusting God, ask Him to help you. The Bible says that when you aren't faithful to God, He will still be faithful to you (2 Timothy 2:13).

Dear God, I will trust You. You have always been faithful to me. Everything You do is good, right, and true. Amen.

ARE YOU TRUSTWORTHY?

"Whoever can be trusted with very little can also be trusted with much, and whoever is dishonest with very little will also be dishonest with much."
LUKE 16:10 NIV

When you were little, your parents held your hand so you wouldn't run into the street. You don't need your hand held anymore. Your parents trust you now to watch out for cars and to know when a situation is unsafe. Each day, your parents trust you to be more responsible. You are earning their trust. Can you be trusted with little things? Do you always keep your word? How about keeping secrets friends tell you? Can you be trusted to keep your room clean and help with chores without being asked? When you prove that you are trustworthy with little things, then people will know they can trust you with even more. You earn trust with God too. When He sees He can trust you with things like making right choices and caring for others, then He will trust you with bigger things.

Dear God, I want to be someone who is trustworthy. I will do my best to earn Your trust. Amen.

TRUSTING OTHERS

In time of trouble, trusting in a man who is not faithful is like a bad tooth or a foot out of joint.
PROVERBS 25:19 NLV

A toothache, sore foot, or pain in any other part of your body isn't fun. When someone treats you badly, your heart can hurt too. Heartache makes you feel sad and even unsure of yourself. We expect people to be kind and treat us well. We believe we can trust our friends to love and care for us. If someone treats us badly again and again, then they betray our trust. It's good to be wise when choosing your friends. A good friend will be honest, kind, and caring. She will stand up for you in good times and in bad. Maybe you have friends like that, friends you know you can trust. You have another friend, a best friend—God! He is the most trustworthy friend of all. Wherever you go, whatever you do, in the best and worst of times, God will be with you. He will protect you and help you to be strong.

Dear God, thank You for being my most trustworthy friend. Amen.

I HOPE. . .

Love hopes for all things.
1 CORINTHIANS 13:7 NLV

Hope is wanting something to happen or wanting something to be true. When you pray, you hope to receive what you ask for. But what if you don't? What if God says no or makes you wait? Would you lose hope and stop trusting in Him? Losing hope often means giving up, and that's not what God wants. Instead, you should keep hoping and trusting that God is working on a great plan for your life. Maybe you aren't ready to receive what you hope for, or maybe God has something even better waiting for you up ahead. Hope means still having faith in God when you don't get what you want. It means having patience. You can trust God; you already know that. God hears what you ask for when you pray. He knows what you hope for. Put your hope in Him because He promises to help you all through your life and to love you in a way no one else can.

Dear God, I will put my hope in You and expect You to give me exactly what I need. Amen.

IN YOUR DREAMS

"'For I know the plans I have for you,' says the Lord, 'plans for well-being and not for trouble, to give you a future and a hope.'"
JEREMIAH 29:11 NLV

In Jeremiah 29:11, God promises that He has plans for you. His plans for your future are good, and He wants you to look forward to your future with hope. Right now you might be dreaming about where you'd like to live when you grow up. Maybe you wonder if you will get married and have kids. When you think about a career, you might dream of being a veterinarian, a doctor, a youth pastor, a beautician, a store owner, or something else. You can't know what God has planned for you. But take a look at the things you are good at. God gave you those things for a reason. They will be the foundation on which you will build your future. What would you like to do when you grow up? Where do you think God will lead you?

Dear God, I'm ready for You to lead me into the future. Show me the way. Amen.

HIDDEN IN MY HEART

Your Word have I hid in my heart, that I may not sin against You.
PSALM 119:11 NLV

The Bible is filled with God's promises—more than three thousand of them! As you read your Bible, you will discover some of them. Along with God's promises, you will learn what God expects from you. You will also begin to understand who God is and the power He has over everyone and everything. Reading the Bible isn't enough. It's important to remember its words and put them to use every day. Challenge yourself to memorize a certain number of Bible verses each week. When you memorize a verse, put it to work and see if it makes a difference in what you do or how you get along with others. Here's one to get you started: "Children, obey your parents in everything. The Lord is pleased when you do" (Colossians 3:20 NLV). The more you hide God's Word in your heart, the more prepared you will be to deal with whatever comes your way.

Dear God, I will memorize Bible verses and think about them. Help me to put them into action. Amen.

PARENTS

"For God said, 'Show respect to your father and mother.'"
MATTHEW 15:4 NLV

Parents love their kids in many different ways. You've already learned about some of them. Love is patient. Love is kind. It's unselfish. It puts others before itself. Love doesn't get angry easily, and it doesn't keep track of how many times someone messes up. Love isn't happy when it sees someone doing what's wrong. It likes the truth. Love protects, trusts, and hopes. Best of all, love never gives up. Do you see your parents loving you in these ways? God gave your parents the important job of loving you and helping you to grow up. Their decisions might not always be easy for you to understand, but if your parents trust God to help them guide you, then you know they are doing the best they can. Your job is to trust that your mom and dad are doing what they think is right for you. So remember to respect them even when you don't like what they do.

Dear God, thank You for my parents, and forgive me for not always respecting their rules. Amen.

SIBLINGS

We must not be proud or make trouble with each other or be jealous of each other.

GALATIANS 5:26 NCV

Some Bible stories show siblings behaving badly. Cain was jealous of his younger brother, Abel. Esau was jealous of his younger brother, Jacob. Joseph's older brothers were so jealous they sold Joseph as a slave! God wasn't pleased when older siblings made trouble for younger ones and didn't get along. When a new baby is born into a family and everyone's attention shifts to the baby, older brothers and sisters can become jealous. That's when trouble starts. Maybe you are the oldest in your family. God has given you the important job of helping your younger sisters or brothers grow up. You've had those experiences that are new to them, and you understand better than anyone what they are thinking and how they feel. So instead of being jealous of your younger siblings, be their role model. It pleases God to see you helping them and showing them loving-kindness.

Dear God, forgive me for any jealous feelings I have toward my siblings. I'll do my best to always be loving and kind. Amen.

GRANDPARENTS

Old people are proud of their grandchildren,
and children are proud of their parents.
PROVERBS 17:6 NCV

Grandparents are some of the coolest people on the planet. They are so proud of their grandchildren, and they love to show them off and brag about them to their friends. Grandparents are first in line to want the latest school pictures, and they can't wait for their grandchildren to call them or video chat. One of the neatest things about grandparents is they have endless stories to tell. Not the kind of stories you read in books, but stories about their lives. Grandparents have lived a long time, and they are very wise. So ask them lots of questions. Encourage them to tell you about what it was like to grow up long ago and what helped them get through hard times. God gave you grandparents to teach you important lessons about life. The Bible tells grandparents to teach you what they know about God (Deuteronomy 4:9). Do you have grandparents? What is your most favorite thing about each one?

Dear God, thank You for my grandparents.
Remind me to spend time with them
and talk with them. Amen.

FRIENDS

A friend loves at all times.
PROVERBS 17:17 NLV

You can't know everything God has planned for your future, but you can be sure of this—God will give you friends. Good friends are a gift from God. The friends you have now are just a few of the many friends you will have throughout your life. God brings friends into our lives exactly when we need them and for a purpose. Friends bring us joy. They add fun to our lives and make us laugh. Friends are helpers. When we feel sad, they help us feel better. If a project is too hard or too big to do alone, friends help with that too. Good friends are like cheerleaders. They love us, encourage us, and are happy for us when we accomplish our goals. Some of the friends you have right now might be in your life forever. Other friends you haven't met yet. God has them waiting for you in the future, and He will bring them to you when the time is just right.

Dear God, I'm excited to meet the new friends You have planned for me. Thank You for my friends. Amen.

FRIENDS ARE EVERYWHERE

A man who has friends must be a friend.
PROVERBS 18:24 NLV

The friends you have right now are probably kids you met in school, at church, or in your neighborhood. Maybe your friends' parents are friends of your parents and that's how you met. Some friends you met because you're on the same sports team or you share another activity. Are you ready to make even more friends? Instead of waiting for them to find you, you can find them! Say hello to the new girl. Invite her to have fun with you. Maybe there's a girl you know who's super crafty. Don't be shy. Tell her you love what she makes. Maybe she can teach you how to make it too. To find new friends, you have to be a friend, and that means making the first move. Ask questions to show you're interested to learn more about someone. Give compliments. Offer to help. Go someplace new and try new things. You never know when or where you'll find a friend.

Dear God, sometimes I'm shy about meeting new people. Please help me to welcome new friends into my life. Amen.

SHE'S SO DIFFERENT!

The rich and the poor meet together.
The Lord is the maker of them all.
PROVERBS 22:2 NLV

God made each of us to be one of a kind. Even identical twins are different. On the outside they might look alike, but inside each is a special person created by God with a purpose. How do you choose new friends? Do you always look for friends who are most like you? It's good to have friends who share the same things you do. But friends who are different can be some of the best friends of all. They can show you what it's like to live in different cities, states, and countries, or what it's like to live in a family that's different from yours. They can teach you about cultures and traditions that are unfamiliar to you. If someone doesn't look like you or speak the way you do, that shouldn't stop you from being their friend. God made us all. He wants us to get to know one another and treat each other with love and respect.

Dear God, thank You for my friends.
Each is one of a kind and special. Amen.

GODLY FRIENDS

The righteous choose their friends carefully,
but the way of the wicked leads them astray.
PROVERBS 12:26 NIV

A godly friend is someone who knows and trusts God and does her best to follow His rules. Godly friends are alike in one very special way—they love Jesus! Godly friends help each other grow nearer to God. They pray, encourage, and help each other. They are good listeners. They tell each other the truth, and they are kind and unselfish. Instead of being jealous, they are each other's best cheerleaders. A godly friend is loyal. That means she won't go off with other friends and leave you behind. She will do her best to make sure you aren't alone. No one is perfect. If a godly friend hurts your feelings or otherwise lets you down, she is quick to apologize and make things right. Godly friends forgive one another. They bring out the best in you because they help you become more like Jesus. Do you have godly friends?

Dear God, I want my closest friends to be godly friends. Please help me to be that kind of friend too. Amen.

YES, YOU CAN!

Therefore encourage one another and build each other up, just as in fact you are doing.
1 THESSALONIANS 5:11 NIV

Your friend is planning to walk with her dad in a charity walk for a local animal shelter. It's a 10K (six-mile) walk. She and her dad planned that they would walk the first 5K (three miles) together, and he will walk the last three miles alone. But your friend told you a secret. She plans to walk the whole 10K! Because you are an awesome, godly friend, you encourage her and help her train. At recess you walk with her, doing laps around the playground. You encourage her to eat healthy, and you ask questions to show you care. If she says, "I'm not sure I can do it," you answer, "Yes, you can!" You encourage your friend to share her secret with her mom so it won't come as a total surprise when after 5K she keeps going. Friends encourage one another in all things. They especially encourage each other to do what is good, right, and pleasing to God.

Dear God, teach me how to be a good encourager. Amen.

A FRIEND TO ANIMALS

"A man who is right with God cares for his animal."
PROVERBS 12:10 NLV

When God created the earth, He said, "Let Us make man like Us and let him be head over the fish of the sea, and over the birds of the air, and over the cattle. . .and over every thing that moves on the ground" (Genesis 1:26 NLV). God put the first man, Adam, in charge of caring for the animals. Would you like to help care for them too? Learn about the wild animals that live in your area. Maybe your family or youth group at church can create a wildlife habitat with plants that give birds and small animals a place to eat, hide, and nest. You can help pets that have no home by donating pet food and other supplies to your local animal shelters. And, of course, you are a best friend to your own pets. They rely on you for everything. Can you think of more ways to be a friend to God's animals?

Dear God, please give me some ideas for how to help and care for Your animals. Amen.

BE A GODLY HELPER

Christian brothers, if a person is found doing some sin, you who are stronger Christians should lead that one back into the right way. Do not be proud as you do it. Watch yourself, because you may be tempted also.

GALATIANS 6:1 NLV

Imagine that your best friend messed up and did something she knew was wrong. She told you about it, and you agreed that it was wrong. Your friend can't decide whether to keep what she did a secret or tell her parents. What advice would you give her? Galatians 6:1 can help. If you know your friend did something wrong, you should encourage her to take responsibility and do what she can to make it right. When you encourage her, do it gently. Be kind and choose the best words. Encouraging isn't blaming or scolding. Instead, it's reminding your friend about what God would want her to do.

Dear God, show me how to encourage my friends to do what's right, not because I'm better than them but because it's right for us to remind each other to do what pleases You. Amen.

GOOD ADVICE

Listen to advice and accept correction,
and in the end you will be wise.
PROVERBS 19:20 NCV

Are you troubled about something but you haven't told anyone? It's never wrong to share your troubles and ask for advice. Your parents, grandparents, teachers, pastors, and other trusted adults give good advice. Friends can help too. Friends might understand better than a grown-up what's worrying you and how you feel. Sometimes talking things over with your best friend can help, and talking with God *always* helps. God already knows what's troubling you, and He knows the way to lead you out of your trouble. The Bible gives perfect advice. The more you read and study it, the better you will know how to handle your problems. Reading the Bible will make you wise. You will learn what God expects from you and how His power can work in you to help when trouble comes your way. If you needed some advice today, who is the first person you would ask?

Dear God, I need some wise advice. You know what's troubling me. Please lead me to those who can help. Show me what to do. Amen.

MUSCLES

He gives strength to the weak. And He gives power to him who has little strength.

ISAIAH 40:29 NLV

Maybe you and your family moved to a new home and used a moving company to help. It takes strength to lift heavy furniture. It takes endurance too—the ability to keep going. You need strong arms and legs to pick up and carry heavy things. But muscles aren't the only way to be strong. There is another kind of strength. Faith in God gives you strength to say, "Yes, I can," when that little voice in your head says, *No, you can't*. Isaiah 40:29 is another of God's promises. When you think you can't do something because you aren't good enough or smart enough, or for any other reason, God promises to give you the power to try and keep on trying. God promises to give you strength whenever you feel weak. Gaining strong muscles requires working out and staying in shape. God's kind of strength requires just one thing—that you put all your faith and trust in Him.

Dear God, give me strength and Your power to do these things I think I can't. Amen.

FAITH

Now faith is being sure we will get what we hope for. It is being sure of what we cannot see.

HEBREWS 11:1 NLV

What if people kept saying, "You can't"? What if they said you can't because you don't know enough or you aren't creative enough or patient enough or strong enough? All those "not enoughs" would deflate your self-esteem like air rushing from a popped balloon! Faith is believing that you *are* good enough. You are good enough because God says you are, and God always speaks the truth. When you see yourself as weak and not able to do something, God sees you tapping into His power and His strength and fighting whatever gets in your way. When you see yourself giving up hope of reaching your goals, God sees you racing for the finish line shouting, "Yes, I can!" Faith is seeing yourself through God's eyes. Faith is trusting in His love for you and knowing that whenever you feel weak or unsure of yourself, He will help you to become sure and strong.

Dear God, I can do just about anything when I put my faith in You. Amen.

Faith Building

Now the God Who helps you not to give up and gives you strength will help you think so you can please each other as Christ Jesus did.

Romans 15:5 NLV

Faith means stepping out of your comfort zone. It's the willingness to try new things. Remember, God promises to help you. Maybe you're worried about singing in front of people or climbing that rock wall at the gym. If you give it a try while remembering God is with you, He will help you to get rid of your fear. What new thing would you like to try today? When you learn to put your faith in God and become comfortable trying new things, then you can help other kids build their faith too. You do that by encouraging them to try and by being their helper so they don't have to try alone. You can help build their faith by sharing with them God's promise that He will give them strength to try and not give up. Do you know someone who could use some faith-building help?

Dear God, please help me to help others put their faith and trust in You. Amen.

A LITTLE HELP, PLEASE

Say to those whose heart is afraid, "Have strength of heart, and do not be afraid. See, your God will come. . . . He will save you."
ISAIAH 35:4 NLV

Can you imagine someone trying to carry a sofa or refrigerator to a moving van all by himself? A helper is needed to carry big things. The same is true when you have a big problem. Often you'll need a friend to help boost your strength. If your problem is schoolwork, your teacher can help you. If you're afraid of learning to swim, a grown-up can teach you and help you feel confident and safe. If you don't enjoy going to new places and meeting people, a friend can go along to help you feel more comfortable. God gives us helpers. When you don't feel very strong, a friend can be strong for you. You can be a strength booster too. If you knew someone was worried or afraid, what could you do to help?

Dear God, when a problem seems too big for me to handle alone, thank You for those who help boost my strength. Amen.

DON'T GIVE UP

"I have prayed for you. I have prayed that your faith will be strong and that you will not give up."
LUKE 22:32 NLV

Some of your friends don't know Jesus. If you talk about believing in Jesus or about knowing right from wrong, they might think you are different or strange. After a while, you could feel like giving up and not mentioning Jesus at all. Even worse, you might give up doing what God wants and instead join in with what your friends want. Jesus is speaking in today's verse. He tells one of His disciples, "Satan has wanted to have you. . . . But I have prayed for you. I have prayed that your faith will be strong and that you will not give up" (Luke 22:31–32 NLV). Imagine Jesus saying those words to you when you feel like giving up on Him. Jesus wants your faith to remain strong. If your friends don't like that you believe in and obey Jesus, pray for them, and ask your Christian friends to pray for you that your faith remains strong.

Dear Jesus, I pray that all my friends will know and love You. Amen.

IS IT RIGHT OR WRONG?

Do not let anyone fool you. Bad people can make those who want to live good become bad.
1 CORINTHIANS 15:33 NLV

Who is your best friend? Did you say, "Jesus"? He is the best friend you will ever have. If you follow Him and try to be like Him, you will live in a way that pleases God. Be careful that none of your friends leads you away from Jesus. If a friend made fun of somebody, would you join in? What if a friend was swearing and using God's or Jesus' name? Would you start using that kind of language? If you remember that Jesus is your best friend, it will be easier to say no. If you're unsure whether something is right or wrong, then it's probably not something you should do right away. You can pray and ask Jesus to help you. And you already know adults who can help you decide what's right or wrong. Don't let anyone fool you into thinking that something is right when you know God wouldn't approve.

Dear Jesus, please help me always to choose right over wrong. Amen.

WELCOME!

Receive each other as Christ received you. This will honor God.

ROMANS 15:7 NLV

Do you have a friend who is more like a sister? It's fun having a best friend. A best friend is someone you share secrets with. She knows you so well! The two of you hang out all the time, doing all kinds of fun things together. A best friend is great to have, but if you spend all your time with just one special friend, you're missing out on a lot. Each friend you welcome into your life brings new ideas and new things for you to explore and be interested in. Each has something special to bring into your friendship. You honor God when you welcome new friends. Inviting more friends into your circle is something you and your best friend can do together. You could think of yourselves as Team Jesus, working together to welcome girls who have few friends or the new kids at your church or school.

Dear God, thank You for my best friend. Lead me to welcome many good friends into my life. Amen.

QUIET TIME

Be quiet and know that I am God.

PSALM 46:10 NLV

Spending time with family and friends is good. But sometimes you want to be alone. You need some quiet time all by yourself to recharge. When you're by yourself, you might dream about places you want to go, things you would like to see, even what you want to do when you're older. Or you might spend quiet time reading a book, drawing, writing, or learning something new. When you are alone someplace quiet, that's the perfect time to read your Bible and learn more about God. It's also the perfect time to pray. Remember that prayer is more than just asking God for things. It's telling Him about how your day went, any concerns you have, your hopes and dreams, and your thoughts about—everything! God loves meeting you in the quiet and listening to you without any interruptions. How do you like to spend quiet time? What would you like to talk with God about today?

Dear God, let's meet for a while in a quiet place. I have so much to tell You, and I know You are waiting for me. Amen.

GOD HEARS ME

We are sure that if we ask anything that He wants us to have, He will hear us.

1 John 5:14 NLV

Whenever you pray, even if it's a tiny prayer like "Please help me," God hears. God hears all your prayers whether you say them aloud or to yourself. A prayer doesn't have to be perfect. You don't have to say special words or put words together in just the right way. You don't have to go to church or someplace special to say your prayers. God is with you all the time wherever you go. It isn't just your prayers God listens to. He hears every word you say. God loves it when you want to talk with Him, and He is never too busy to spend time with you. Even before you tell Him, God knows if something is troubling you, and He is ready to help. He knows what you want before you ask for it, and He is always ready to give you exactly what you need.

Dear God, whether I pray out loud
or quietly inside my heart,
I know that You hear me. Amen.

PRAYER IS MY GPS

May the lifting up of my hands be like the evening gift given on the altar in worship.
PSALM 141:2 NLV

If you're traveling, the GPS on a phone works like a compass pointing you in the right direction. Prayer is like a GPS because it points you toward God. You can imagine your words zooming right up to heaven and into God's ears! Some prayers are short; others are long. You don't have to think of exactly what to say ahead of time; the words will come. Just start. God will guide you. If you are planning to spend some time talking with God, you can begin by worshipping Him. That means telling God you know how great He is and that you are respectful of all He is and everything He does. It means thanking Him for your blessings. When you worship God, you might even lift your hands up toward heaven. That's another way of showing that you want to come even nearer to Him. Prayer connects you with God, and if you follow the path He has set for you, you won't get lost.

Dear God, lead me in the right direction. Amen.

PLEASE FORGIVE ME

If we tell [God] our sins, He is faithful and we can depend on Him to forgive us of our sins. He will make our lives clean from all sin.

1 JOHN 1:9 NLV

Other than Jesus, no one on earth has ever been perfect. From the beginning, people have done things to displease God. Even the first humans, Adam and Eve, messed up. God gave them a perfect garden to live in. They had just one rule: Don't eat fruit from "the tree of learning of good and bad" (Genesis 2:17 NLV). But they disobeyed, and that caused sin to enter God's perfect world. The Bible says if we ask for God's forgiveness for the wrong things we do, we can depend on Him to forgive us. He will wash away what we've done as if it never happened. When you pray, don't hide what you've done wrong. God already knows. Talk with Him about it and ask for His forgiveness. First John 1:9 is another of His promises. You can always count on God to forgive you.

Dear God, I know You saw how I messed up today. I'm sure it displeased You. Please forgive me. Amen.

ASK QUESTIONS

If you do not have wisdom, ask God for it. He is always ready to give it to you and will never say you are wrong for asking.

JAMES 1:5 NLV

God wants you to ask Him questions when you pray. One thing you can ask for is wisdom. You become wiser when you ask God to guide you, listen to His words, and follow His rules. You can say things like "God, how can I get myself out of this trouble?" or "Where are You leading me?" or "What are You trying to teach me?" You can ask, "Lord, what do You want me to do?" or "Father, will You help me make the right choice?" And when you are asking God to do things for you, remember also to ask what you can do for Him or for others. "Father, what can I offer You?" "God, how can I help my friend?" When you ask God questions, expect Him to answer. He promises to give you wisdom if you ask.

Dear God, I'm not sure what to do. Where are You leading me? Which way do You want me to go? Amen.

WHAT SHOULD I PRAY ABOUT?

Learn to pray about everything. Give thanks to God as you ask Him for what you need.
PHILIPPIANS 4:6 NLV

What do you want? Maybe you want more freedom to do things you believe you're old enough to do. Or maybe there's someplace you'd like to visit or a new activity you really want to try. Talk with God about it. If you're worried or afraid, you can talk with Him about that too. What if a family member or friend is sick? Tell God. There's nothing you can't talk with Him about. The Bible says to pray about everything. Prayer goes way beyond asking God for stuff. It's talking with Him as you would your closest friend. It's trusting Him to keep your secrets and help with all your troubles. Can you list three questions you want to ask Him? Three people you'd like to pray for? How about three wishes or dreams you have?

Dear God, I have so many things to talk with You about today. Thank You for always having time for me and wanting to hear my prayers. Amen.

ONE STEP AHEAD

"And it will be before they call, I will answer. While they are still speaking, I will hear."
ISAIAH 65:24 NLV

Try this with a friend. See if each of you can guess what the other is thinking. Try it three times. How many times did you and your friend guess right? You can't know what someone is thinking—but God can! God is always one step ahead of you. He knows your thoughts before you think them, and He knows your questions before you ask. God knows ahead of time the people you will meet, the words you will say, and the choices you will make. Because God already knows, He is able to guide you in the right direction. God made you. He has your whole life planned. He knows your future. When you come to Him in prayer, you can be sure nothing you say will surprise Him. God knows what you will ask for, and He already has an answer.

Dear God, You know me better than anyone else. You made me, and I'm grateful for the plans You have for me. Amen.

CONFIDENCE!

Let us then approach God's throne of grace with confidence, so that we may receive mercy and find grace to help us in our time of need.

HEBREWS 4:16 NIV

Confidence means believing with your whole heart that you can trust in someone or something. Because your parents love you, you trust they will take good care of you. Every day since the beginning of time the sun has risen and set, so you are sure that it will happen again tomorrow. You can have confidence in yourself too. You can be sure you will do well on the next spelling test because you studied hard and you're an expert speller. The Bible says we should come to God in prayer with confidence. You can be confident that God will always be ready to listen to your prayers and that He will forgive your sins. You can be certain He will help with whatever trouble you have. Can you think of three other things about God that you believe with your whole heart?

Dear God, I am confident that You love me. I have confidence that You hear my prayers and will answer them. Amen.

READ, LEARN, REPEAT

"Get your life from Me and I will live in you."

JOHN 15:4 NLV

How many Bible verses have you memorized? If you said, "Too many to count," good for you! Memorizing scripture is a great way to put God's words into action. Everything in the Bible is true. So when you memorize Bible verses, you are remembering God's promises. If your parents allow you to use the internet, you can search for topics in the Bible. You can find Bible verses to help when you have a decision to make or when you are worried or afraid. You can memorize Bible verses that help when someone hurts your feelings or when you need to forgive. When you have memorized a verse, talk with God about it when you pray. Repeat the Bible verse to Him, and ask Him to help you understand and put it to use in your life. Try this: Have a contest with your parents and siblings. See who knows the most Bible verses. Challenge each other to learn even more.

Dear God, thank You for the Bible. Please help me to memorize its words and put them to use. Amen.

PSALM TWENTY-THREE

The Lord is my Shepherd. I will have everything I need.

PSALM 23:1 NLV

King David, the Bible's most famous king, wrote Psalm 23. (A psalm is a song or poem meant to worship and praise God.) David said that God is like a good shepherd who cares for his sheep. Think about it. God gives you everything you need. He gives you peaceful, quiet places where you can rest. God's good care makes you strong. He helps you do what is right, and when you obey Him, He is pleased. When trouble comes, even really bad stuff, God stays with you and helps you. You don't have to be afraid, because God will never leave you. Knowing He is always with you and cares for you gives you a feeling of comfort. If someone treats you badly, you can count on God to love you and pour His blessings into your life. Read and memorize Psalm 23. It's a great one to remember whenever you're worried or afraid.

Dear God, I like thinking of You as a kind and loving shepherd who protects me. I feel safe and loved in Your care. Amen.

THE LORD'S PRAYER

Our Father in heaven, help us to honor your name.

MATTHEW 6:9 CEV

Jesus was on a mountainside speaking to a huge crowd. He taught them many things, including how to pray. When you go to your quiet place to talk with God, if the words don't come, you can use Jesus' prayer—the Lord's Prayer—as a model to get you started. Read His prayer in your Bible in Matthew 6:9–13. You can memorize and pray those exact words, or you could say something like this: "My heavenly Father, help me to honor Your name. Come and set up Your kingdom so that everyone on earth will obey You as You are obeyed in heaven. Give me what I need for today. Forgive me for doing wrong, and guide me to forgive others. Keep me from being tempted to do what I know is wrong, and protect me from evil. Your power and greatness will last forever. Amen." If you don't know what to say to God, the Lord's Prayer is the best one to say.

Dear Jesus, thank You for teaching me Your prayer. I will memorize it and say it to God. Amen.

PRAY TOGETHER

These all agreed as they prayed together.
ACTS 1:14 NLV

In church the pastor sometimes leads a prayer with people joining in saying the words. Group prayer is good because it brings God's people together. Maybe your family prays together before a meal. Praying together isn't always everyone saying the same prayer aloud. It's also a way to pray for others. Ask your parents if one night a week your family can spend some time praying together. You could begin by praying aloud Psalm 23 or the Lord's Prayer. Then pray for one another's needs. Maybe your brother needs prayer to heal the knee he hurt playing soccer. Maybe your mom needs prayerful encouragement for a charity event she's planning. Maybe you need prayer for a test at school. Ask family members what they need, and then have each family member say a short prayer aloud, asking God to meet that need. Get in the habit of praying together and for one another. It will bring your family closer and lead you nearer to God.

Dear God, we welcome You into our home. Please hear our prayers as we pray for one another. Amen.

PRAISE GOD!

I will give thanks to the Lord because He is right and good.
I will sing praise to the name of the Lord Most High.

PSALM 7:17 NLV

God is so wonderful. Can you think of a few ways that God is great? King David thought a lot about God's greatness. He wanted to express his thankfulness to God, so he wrote psalms—poems and songs of praise. In church we sing hymns and praise songs. Music is one way we praise God. Praising Him through words and music is our way of thanking Him for all the blessings in our lives. The Bible commands everything to praise the Lord. Not just people, but angels, the sun, moon, stars, animals, sea creatures, birds, and trees all praise the Lord. Read in your Bible Psalm 148 to find out who and what praises God. Try writing your very own praise song or poem thanking God. It doesn't have to be perfect. God will love whatever you come up with. Say your poem aloud or sing your song to Him.

Dear God, I praise You for Your greatness and for all the ways You bless me. Amen.

COMPLIMENTS

Let another man praise you, and not your own mouth. Let a stranger, and not your own lips.
PROVERBS 27:2 NLV

"I love your outfit." "Great job!" "I'm so proud of you." It feels good to receive a compliment, doesn't it? When someone says something wonderful about you, it makes you feel even better about yourself. Complimenting family members and friends is one way of showing that you love and respect them. But compliments aren't only for people you know. Maybe your teacher invited a guest to your classroom to give a talk about a topic that interests you. Afterward, you could tell the guest, "I really liked your talk." That's a compliment. You could also compliment your teacher: "You're the best teacher ever for inviting Mr. _____ to visit us." Giving compliments is pleasing to God because it shows we care about one another. Compliments help others feel good about themselves. Look for something good in everyone you meet, and when you've found it, turn it into a compliment.

Dear God, remind me to give compliments. You are honored when I see the good in others and let them know. Amen.

CONVERSATION STARTERS

Do not always be thinking about your own plans only.
Be happy to know what other people are doing.
PHILIPPIANS 2:4 NLV

The Bible reminds us not to be thinking of ourselves so much that we aren't interested in others. When you meet new people, you can get to know them by asking questions and being interested in their answers. You might be a little shy. Maybe you don't know what to say. Here are some conversation starters: "Have you ever been to a concert?" "Do you like school?" "Do you have any pets?" "Do you go to church?" "Have you ever played soccer?" "Did you always live in this city?" "Do your grandparents live nearby?" "How many brothers and sisters do you have?" "Does your family like to camp?" You can probably think of many more questions to ask. Each question is a building block in a conversation. Be happy to know what other people are doing. Your first conversation with someone might lead you to make a new friend.

Dear God, remind me not to think only of myself but to be interested in others. Amen.

TOUGH QUESTIONS

Plans go wrong without talking together, but they will go well when many wise men talk about what to do.
PROVERBS 15:22 NLV

If something is bothering a family member or friend, do you notice? If your little brother is having a tantrum or if he's lying on his bed crying, you know he's angry and sad. Sometimes, it's easy to tell how a person is feeling. But other times it's not. Maybe something is bothering you. You haven't told anyone, but those who know you well might see you're much quieter than usual. Your mom or best friend might ask, "Are you okay?" It helps when others notice you aren't yourself and ask if you're all right. "Why are you sad?" "Can I help you not feel so angry?" "Did something bad happen to you?" Some questions are tough to ask because they are about unhappy things. But tough questions show that you care. If those you love are a little quieter than usual, if their faces look angry or sad, don't be afraid to ask if they are okay.

Dear God, help me to notice and care about how others might be feeling. Amen.

BE A GOOD LISTENER

A fool does not find joy in understanding,
but only in letting his own mind be known.
PROVERBS 18:2 NLV

Maybe when you were younger your mom reminded you, "Listen to my words." It's important to listen to what others say. When you really listen, you show you care. Listening is more than just hearing. A good listener thinks about the words she hears. She tries to understand, and if she doesn't, she asks questions. Good listening leads to good learning. When you pay attention to what your teacher says and ask questions, you will do better in school. When you listen to your parents' words and think about what they're trying to teach you, you'll get along better with them too. Practice being a good listener. Let others finish speaking before you speak. Think about their words. Good listening takes practice, but when you become a good listener, others will notice. They'll know that because you care, they can come to you and talk about what's concerning them.

Dear God, good listening shows others I care about their words. Guide me to become a good and caring listener. Amen.

LISTENING TO GOD

"My sheep hear My voice and I know them. They follow Me."
JOHN 10:27 NLV

When you have a conversation with someone, you talk and listen. That's how it should be when you pray. Prayer is talking and listening. Jesus said, "My sheep [the people who know Me] hear My voice." When talking with God, you won't hear His voice speaking aloud, but you can hear Him inside your heart. Part of having a conversation with God is being quiet. Sometimes in the quietness, you will get a feeling in your heart of what God wants you to do, or about something He wants you to learn or know. You can ask Him to guide your thinking. If you have a decision to make, ask God to help you. When you have a problem, ask Him to help you work through it. You won't get the feeling of God speaking to you every time you pray, but after a while you'll learn to recognize His voice in your heart. When you spend time with God, remember to sit quietly sometimes and listen.

Dear God, please help me to hear
Your voice in my heart. Amen.

IS THAT YOU, GOD?

For the Word of the Lord is right. He is faithful in all He does.

PSALM 33:4 NLV

When you have a feeling inside your heart telling you to do something, is it always God speaking to you? No, it isn't. When God speaks inside your heart, He will lead you in the right direction. If you get a feeling that it's okay to disobey your parents, lie, take something that doesn't belong to you, or follow a friend doing what you know is wrong, that feeling doesn't come from God. As you read and study the Bible, you learn what God says is right and wrong. You learn what God expects from you. If the feeling in your heart lines up with what the Bible says, then you're on the right path. But if it doesn't, don't follow it. The Bible is another way God speaks to you. Its words are always right and true. God's voice inside your heart will never lead you away from it.

Dear God, teach me to know when a thought or feeling inside my heart comes from You. Amen.

FAITHFUL FRIEND

"No one can have greater love than to give his life for his friends."
JOHN 15:13 NLV

A faithful friend sticks with you, no matter what. You can always trust her to be there for you. You can depend on her to keep her promises and tell you the truth. A faithful friend never says unkind things about you. She is ready to forgive when the two of you have a disagreement. A faithful friend will never leave you. Jesus is the best example of a faithful friend. You can always count on Him to stay with you. He will never lead you the wrong way. He loves and forgives you no matter how many times you mess up. Whenever you are in trouble or have a problem, Jesus will guide you through it. Jesus is so faithful to you that He agreed to take all your sins as His own so you would be able to live with Him forever in heaven. Along with Jesus, do you have other faithful friends?

Dear Jesus, You are the best example of a faithful friend. Teach me to become like You. Amen.

A LITTLE SHY

For God did not give us a spirit of fear. He gave us a spirit of power and of love and of a good mind.

2 TIMOTHY 1:7 NLV

The Bible tells the story of Moses. God chose him to guide God's people, the Israelites, out of Egypt where they were slaves. God told Moses to tell Egypt's leader, "Let My people go!" Moses wasn't happy about his assignment. He wasn't a good speaker, and that made him shy. Moses asked God to send someone else. God said no. He knew Moses could do it. So Moses obeyed God. He not only spoke to that leader, but Moses also led God's people out of Egypt to a new home God had promised them. Maybe, like Moses, you are a little shy. If you're faced with something new and uncomfortable, maybe you want to say, "God, please don't make me do it!" But if you let Him, God will make you strong. When you say no to being shy, God can lead you to do great things.

Dear God, sometimes I'm a little shy. I'm going to be brave and rely on You to make me strong. Amen.

Still Standing

Put on all the things God gives you to fight with. Then you will be able to stand. . . . When it is all over, you will still be standing.
Ephesians 6:13 NLV

When you're afraid to do something, don't worry—God will help you to be brave. God will always be faithful and give you all the tools you need to stand up to fear or shyness or whatever else gets in your way. In the Bible, you can read about the Israelites fighting against their enemies. The enemy army had a giant soldier named Goliath. The Israelites were afraid of him. But God led a young shepherd boy, David, to stand up to that big guy. With just one stone, David knocked Goliath down. David knew if he put all his trust in God, he'd still be standing when the fight ended. Whenever you're afraid, do your best to be brave like David. Stand up to fear instead of running away. God will give you everything you need to keep standing strong.

Dear God, I want to stand strong like David. Teach me to put all my faith and trust in You. Amen.

THE LORD'S STRENGTH

Be strong with the Lord's strength. Put on the things God gives you to fight with. Then you will not fall into the traps of the devil.
EPHESIANS 6:10–11 NLV

When something gets in the way of you living right, that something doesn't come from God. It comes from the devil. When you recognize one of the devil's traps, you can stay out of it by asking God to give you some of His strength. God's strength gives you power. When your thoughts tell you to do something you know is wrong, before you take one more step, ask God to give you strength to walk away. Maybe you feel like disobeying one of your family's rules. God's strength will help you to be obedient. If angry or bad words are about to escape from your lips, God's strength will silence them. Your strength alone isn't enough. But when you add the Lord's strength to yours, His power will guide you away from the devil's traps.

Dear God, please, I need Your strength today. My own strength isn't enough to fight this wrong thing I want to do. Amen.

SATAN

So give yourselves to God. Stand against the devil and he will run away from you.
JAMES 4:7 NLV

Who is the devil? The Bible sometimes calls him "Satan." He first appears in the Bible as a serpent. (Read more about it in Genesis 3.) When God created the first humans, Adam and Eve, He gave them a perfect garden to live in and care for. They had one rule to follow: Don't eat fruit from "the tree of learning of good and bad" (Genesis 2:17 NLV). But Satan, in the form of a serpent, showed up. He caused Eve and Adam to believe it was okay to disobey God and eat from that tree. When they disobeyed, it was like opening a door and letting out all the evil things that God didn't want them to know about. That was the devil's first trick. He has kept on tricking people into disobeying God. But God is way more powerful than Satan. In the end, God will see to it that the devil gets the punishment he deserves.

Dear God, You have all the power over the devil. Nothing he does can get in Your way. Amen.

TRUTH

Wear a belt of truth around your body.

EPHESIANS 6:14 NLV

When you live right, you become stronger in the good ways you think, act, and feel. You learn to make good choices, and you act in ways that are respectful, fair, responsible, caring, and truthful. Telling the truth is one of God's tools that helps make you strong. Lies come from the devil. The Bible calls the devil "the father of lies." When you don't tell the truth, you fall into one of the devil's traps. Imagine you saw a friend doing something wrong. If your parent asked if you saw it, would you tell the truth, or would you protect your friend and tell a lie? Sometimes, choosing to tell the truth is hard, but the truth is always right and pleasing to God. Ephesians 6:14 reminds you to carry the truth with you all the time. Wear it proudly as you might a beautiful belt made of fine jewels.

Dear God, I try my best to always tell the truth, but when telling the truth is hard, please lead me to do what's right. Amen.

POWER!

Wear a piece of iron over your chest which is being right with God.
EPHESIANS 6:14 NLV

Being right with God means doing your best to please Him by following His rules. Standing up for what's right gives you power over anything that tries to pull you away from God. The Bible talks about "the fire-arrows of the devil" (Ephesians 6:16 NLV). These aren't real arrows, sticks with sharp points at the end. The devil's arrows are all the things he does to try to get you to turn away from God. All the time, the devil will try to get you to disobey and displease God. When you feel like doing something wrong, that's the devil firing one of his arrows at you. You don't have to worry though. God will give you some of His power to stop the arrows from hurting you. When God lends you His power, it's like you have a vest made of iron across your chest. It protects your heart from the devil getting in there and messing things up.

Dear God, please give me some of Your power to keep me from doing wrong. Amen.

THE GOOD NEWS OF PEACE

Wear shoes on your feet which are the Good News of peace.
EPHESIANS 6:15 NLV

If you really want to stand up to the devil, spread some peace around. Put on your walking shoes and, wherever you go, bring peace along with you. The devil hates peace. He loves when people are angry with each other. He loves when people argue and say bad things about others. Swear words, especially those that use God's name, are like music to the devil's ears. He wants everyone to run away when they feel afraid, and he loves it when they fail or don't even try. The devil hates Jesus. He doesn't want you telling your friends the good news that Jesus took the punishment for the bad things we do and invited us to live with Him in heaven. God is pleased when you stand up to the devil. You shouldn't be afraid to stand up to him. You have all of God's power and strength protecting you.

Dear God, I won't run away if the devil tries to get in my way. I know You'll protect me wherever I go. Amen.

A COVERING OF FAITH

Most important of all, you need a covering of faith in front of you.
EPHESIANS 6:16 NLV

If you visit a zoo, you'll see strong glass walls separating you from some of the most dangerous animals, animals like lions, tigers, and gorillas. You'll hear the mighty lion's roar like thunder coming from the other side of the glass. When the tiger paces back and forth, stops, looks you right in the eyes, and growls, you aren't afraid. There's a strong wall protecting you. When the gorilla stands up straight and tall and pounds on the glass with his powerful fists, you watch, knowing you are safe with the glass wall between you and him. Having strong faith in God's power is like having a wall of protection between you and everything that might hurt you. You can see and hear everything on the other side of that wall, but faith makes you sure that God's power will protect you. Do you feel God's power all around you? It's there. You can be sure of it.

Dear God, I trust You. My faith in Your strength and power keeps me safe and sound. Amen.

GOD'S WORD

God's Word gives us strength and hope.

ROMANS 15:4 NLV

The Bible is also called "God's Word." It is a collection of ancient books that teach us about God. God speaks to us through its words. The Bible gives us strength and hope. It teaches us right from wrong. It's filled with stories about people who obeyed God and some who didn't. Just like everyone alive today, the people in the Bible weren't perfect. They made mistakes. We can learn from their mistakes what God expects from us and what we should do to please Him. The Bible is divided into two main parts, the Old and New Testaments. The Old Testament talks about before Jesus was born. The New Testament tells us Jesus' story. It includes what some of Jesus' followers wrote after Jesus died. Their words encourage us to live right and share Jesus' story with others. How well do you know Jesus? Read the story of His life in Luke 1–24. The Bible is the greatest book of all. Make a habit of reading it every day.

Dear God, thank You for giving us the Bible. Amen.

NOBODY'S PERFECT

Follow my way of thinking as I follow Christ.
1 CORINTHIANS 11:1 NLV

Nobody's perfect, but each of us can do our best, using Jesus as our example. You're an awesome girl. There are so many great things about you! Whenever you are loving, courageous, kind, generous, and caring, you are being like Jesus. When you stand up for what you know is right and when you use your God-given strength and power to fight evil, you are being even more like Him. We all mess up. We all need forgiveness for the mistakes we make. When you forgive those who are mean or hurt you, that's being like Jesus too. There are even more wonderful things about you. You remember that no one is perfect. You treat everyone with the same amount of respect, and that pleases God. As you read about Jesus in your Bible, think about His personality. Think about how He treated others. Then do your best to be like Him. That's about as close to perfection as you can get!

Dear Jesus, everything about You is perfect. I will never be just like You, but I'll do my best to try. Amen.

DIFFICULT PEOPLE

"If you love those who love you, what pay can you expect from that? Sinners also love those who love them."
LUKE 6:32 NLV

Do you love the girl who tells lies about you? Do you love the boy in your class who makes fun of your hair? How about the crabby old man who owns the convenience store and doesn't like kids—do you love him? Jesus said, "Love those who work against you. Do good to those who hate you. Respect and give thanks for those who try to bring bad to you. Pray for those who make it very hard for you" (Luke 6:27–28 NLV). That's what Jesus said, but He also understands that because you aren't perfect, you can't always love everyone all the time. There are different ways to love others. You could do something kind and good for the girl who hates you. You could pray for the boy who makes fun of you. And you could show respect for the man who owns the convenience store. Jesus' kind of love is about treating others with kindness, forgiveness, and grace.

Dear Jesus, help me to be more loving, like You. Amen.

WHAT IS GRACE?

By the grace of God I am what I am.
1 CORINTHIANS 15:10 NIV

Grace is when God pours all His love and blessings over you even though you don't deserve it. Sin came into the world when Adam and Eve obeyed the devil's lie. Sin includes things like lying, stealing, jealousy, hatred, and selfishness. Can you think of more examples of sin? Sin displeases God. Our sinning makes God sad. Imagine yourself taking brightly colored markers and writing all those sin words on a whiteboard. If you think hard, you could probably come up with dozens of words, so many that you might run out of space to write them all. Now imagine yourself wiping that board clean. That's what God does. He wipes clean all the sin in our lives as if it never existed. That's grace! Even though our sins hurt God, He wipes them away. He cleans our hearts of all that sin and allows us to start over. Learn from God how to treat others. When they displease you, be merciful and show them some grace.

Dear God, thank You for Your gift of grace. Amen.

MERCIFUL YOU

"Be merciful, just as your Father is merciful."
LUKE 6:36 NIV

Mercy is when you give the gift of grace to others. You already know that no one is perfect. Your family members and friends will mess up sometimes—and so will you. Your sister might get angry with you and say something like "You're so mean! I don't like you!" Your mom might come home after a bad day at work, and when you ask her to help with your homework, she might say, "Not now!" and walk away. People mess up. They hurt each other's feelings without meaning to. When you are the one whose feelings get hurt, you can choose how to react. You can get angry and say mean things, or you can react with mercy. In your heart, you could forgive your sister for what she said. You could forgive your mom for not giving you the attention you needed. Being merciful means erasing the sins of others. It takes practice, but do your best to try. Be merciful to others the way God is merciful to you.

Dear God, thank You for Your gift of mercy. Amen.

GOSSIP

Gossip is no good! It causes hard feelings and comes between friends.

Proverbs 16:28 CEV

"Emily did a good job on her art project; she deserved to win first place." "I heard that Emily's mom did a lot of Emily's art project. Emily didn't deserve to win." Which of those two statements is gossip? Gossip is repeating a rumor—something that may or may not be true. It's saying not-so-nice things about people behind their backs. The Bible says gossip is sin. It's bad because it hurts feelings and it separates friends. Don't fall into the devil's trap and spread gossip around. If you hear something unkind said about someone, think about it. Sometimes facts get mixed up. Other times gossip is a total lie about someone. It's unkind to pass gossip around. If you hear gossip that makes you think someone is in danger, it's okay to tell your parents or another trusted adult. When a conversation includes gossip about someone, do your best to turn it around. Say something good about the person. Then move the conversation on to something else.

Dear God, help me to recognize gossip and to stop it from spreading. Amen.

GIRL TALK

Watch your talk! No bad words should be coming from your mouth. Say what is good. Your words should help others grow as Christians.

EPHESIANS 4:29 NLV

God hears every word you say. It isn't only gossip that displeases Him. Any negative speech, arguing, complaining, talk that makes fun of others or puts them down, unkind words, swearing, name-calling—none of it pleases God. Listen to your words. Think before you speak. Are the words you are about to speak good words? Stay away from conversations that include gossip and speaking unkindly about others. Don't swear. God's name should only be used when you are talking respectfully about Him or to Him in prayer. Loud, angry words are never pleasing to God. Instead, use words that are calm and bring peace into angry situations. Good words are like music to God. He loves hearing you speak only kind words about others. He is pleased when you tell the truth and are respectful. He likes hearing you speak gentle, loving words that help others feel good about themselves.

Dear God, I want my words to please You. Amen.

TRUTH AND LIES

The Lord hates lying lips, but those who speak the truth are His joy.
PROVERBS 12:22 NLV

Do you recognize a lie when you hear one? Some lies are so far from truth they are easy to recognize, like when your baby brother says he didn't take a cookie but he has crumbs all over his face. Other lies are disguised so well you might miss them. If you didn't want to clean your room but instead told your mom that you forgot to do it, that's a lie. If you make a promise, knowing you can't keep it, that's a lie too. So is making up stories or parts of stories that you say are the truth. Sometimes people tell lies because the truth is uncomfortable. What if your friend asks if you like her new haircut and you don't? To say you like it would be lying. Can you think of something else you could say that would be kind and not a lie? There are many different ways to lie, and God doesn't like any of them.

Dear God, guide me to recognize lies, and help me not to tell them. Amen.

A QUIET SPIRIT

Your beauty should be a gentle and quiet spirit. In God's sight this is of great worth and no amount of money can buy it.

1 PETER 3:4 NLV

Some things are beautiful on the outside but not on the inside. Maybe you saw a book on the shelf in your school library, and you said to yourself, *What a cool cover!* You loved the art that led you to pick out that book. But when you opened the cover and began reading, you didn't like the story at all. What's on the outside doesn't always match what's on the inside. The same is true with people. Someone who looks beautiful might be not so nice on the inside. The Bible talks about inner beauty. Someone who is beautiful on the inside has a gentle and quiet spirit. Jesus had that kind of spirit. He had a way of making people feel calm when they were with Him. He didn't gossip or cut down people. He led them to live right and feel good about themselves.

Dear Jesus, please teach me to have a gentle and quiet spirit. Amen.

CHECKUP

Put yourselves through a test. See if you belong to Christ. Then you will know you belong to Christ, unless you do not pass the test.
2 CORINTHIANS 13:5 NLV

Maybe you've been with your dad or mom when they took their car for a checkup. The mechanic checked the car's engine, tires, brakes, and other parts to make sure they worked okay. Maybe you've been to a doctor for a checkup. She took your temperature, looked inside your mouth and ears, and checked your heart and lungs to be sure all your parts were working well. There's another kind of checkup you might not have thought of. When was the last time you checked yourself to see if you were living right by obeying God's rules? The Bible says you should put yourself to the test. Give yourself a checkup once in a while. Think about whether you are living in ways that please God. Are you doing your best to become more like Jesus? Are you learning from the Bible what God says is right and wrong?

Dear God, I want all my thoughts and actions to please You. Amen.

WHAT DO YOU SEE?

Anyone who hears the Word of God and does not obey is like a man looking at his face in a mirror. After he sees himself and goes away, he forgets what he looks like.

JAMES 1:23–24 NLV

Have you ever played the game where you have ten seconds to look at a picture and then you have to recall all its details from memory? A brief look at something often isn't enough. When you take a quick glance and then walk away, you might miss seeing something important. The same is true about the Bible. If you just quickly read a verse every day, it's not enough. The Bible is a book you should spend time with. Even if you read just one verse each day, you should spend time thinking about it. A "sister in Christ" is a girlfriend who loves God. Do you have a sister in Christ? Maybe the two of you can read and study the Bible together. The more you read and think about what's in the Bible, the easier it will be for you to obey God.

Dear God, lead me deeper into Your Word. Amen.

FAITH IN ACTION

Do I have to prove to you that faith without doing things is of no use?
JAMES 2:20 NLV

Jesus wants us not only to believe and have faith in Him but also to put His teaching into action. When Jesus lived on earth, many called Him "Rabbi." It's a word that means "teacher." Jesus was the greatest teacher ever. He taught us how God wants us to live. Jesus said we should love each other, even our enemies. We should always be forgiving. When we make promises, we should keep our word. We should be generous, kind, and respectful. He commanded us to love and obey our parents. Jesus said to treat others as we want to be treated. And He reminded us to let our light shine. That means that wherever we go we should serve others and be a good example. Can you think of more things Jesus taught? When you put His teaching into action, others will see, and they might decide to follow Jesus too.

Dear Jesus, teach me. Help me to put into action what I learn. Amen.

Friend Checkup

Do not act like the sinful people of the world. Let God change your life. First of all, let Him give you a new mind. Then you will know what God wants you to do. And the things you do will be good and pleasing and perfect.

ROMANS 12:2 NLV

Examining your friendships is another part of checking yourself to see if you're following Jesus. What are your friends most interested in doing? Has a friend wanted you to try something you know is dangerous or wrong? Do you have friends you can trust to always do what's right? It's good to have many friends, but you should choose your best friends carefully. If you hang out with girls who disobey their teachers and parents, gossip about kids in your class, are mean to others, use bad language, and make fun of people, those girls might lead you away from Jesus. Ask God to give you wisdom when choosing new friends. Ask Him to guide you to friends who love Him and will lead you closer to Jesus.

Dear God, lead me to choose friends You approve of. Amen.

JUDGING OTHERS

"So give Your servant an understanding heart to judge Your people and know the difference between good and bad."
1 KINGS 3:9 NLV

Jesus said, "Do not say what is wrong in other people's lives. Then other people will not say what is wrong in your life" (Matthew 7:1 NLV). That doesn't mean, though, you shouldn't be careful about who you hang out with. It's wrong to judge others by the way they look on the outside, how they dress, how they talk, or where they live. If you judge someone by gossip you heard, that's wrong. You shouldn't judge someone because you believe she's not as smart, pretty, or talented as you. You can tell what someone is like by what's in her heart. The way someone behaves should give you a good idea of what she's like on the inside. When choosing your friends, judge their hearts. Be careful about who you allow into your life. The Bible says don't be with people who do wrong (Proverbs 22:24–25). Choose your friends wisely.

Dear God, help me to surround myself with friends who lead me closer to You. Amen.

THE GOD-PLEASING TEST

Let us test and look over our ways, and return to the Lord.
LAMENTATIONS 3:40 NLV

Keep on testing yourself by thinking about whether what you do and say is pleasing to God. If you are a girl who usually gets 100 percent on tests, be prepared to get a lower grade on the God-pleasing test. Why? Because no one is perfect. Jesus is the only one who would get a perfect score. Do the best you can, and remember that if you mess up, it's okay. You can ask God for forgiveness and for help to do better next time. "The LORD says, 'Forget what happened before, and do not think about the past'" (Isaiah 43:18 NCV). God has forgiven you, and He wants you to forgive yourself and move on. You'll learn from your mistakes how to do better. The God-pleasing test is an open-book test. That means that when you're unsure if your words and behavior are pleasing to God, you can open your Bible and look for the answer there. You can also ask others for help.

Dear God, I will continue testing my behavior to see if it's pleasing to You. Amen.

THE POWERFUL ONE

The Powerful One, God, the Lord, has spoken. And He calls the earth from where the sun rises to where the sun goes down.

PSALM 50:1 NLV

Maybe you know someone who lifts weights. As a beginner, they might lift smaller weights and then add more weight as they improve. Everyone has a limit, though, to how much they can lift. Humans are limited in everything they do. The only one who has no limits is God. He can do anything. God created not just the earth we live on but the entire universe—planets, moons, suns, stars, and everything beyond that we can only imagine. God keeps it all going too. He knows everything about His creation all the time. God can perform great miracles. He parted the water of the Red Sea, making a path so His people, the Israelites, could walk on dry land to the other side. He rained food down from heaven daily to feed His hungry people. He even made the sun and moon stand still. God is all-powerful. There is nothing He cannot do.

Dear God, Your mighty power is amazing. Amen.

GOD, THE CREATOR

"My hands made all these things, and so all these things came into being," says the Lord.

ISAIAH 66:2 NLV

The Bible is the story of God's relationship with His people here on earth. That's not all of His story though. There is so much we don't know and can't know about God. He existed before His story in the Bible begins. God has existed forever, and He will never end. We can only know what He says about Himself and what the Bible tells us. The first words of the Bible say, "In the beginning God made from *nothing* the heavens and the earth" (Genesis 1:1 NLV, italics added). Can you imagine drawing a picture without tools to draw with and a tablet or something else to draw on? If you said, "Picture, draw yourself," would it suddenly appear? Of course not! But that's what God did. He commanded things to happen, and they did. In six days, God spoke His words and commanded our whole world into existence, even everything we see in the sky. God is *that* powerful.

Dear God, You are the only one who can make something from nothing. Amen.

CREATION, DAY ONE

Then God said, "Let there be light," and there was light.

GENESIS 1:3 NLV

Can you think of a time you were in total darkness? Maybe the power went out in your house at night, and everything was totally dark. Or maybe you went camping with your family, and when you went to bed it was so dark in your tent you couldn't see your sister sleeping next to you. The Bible says that in the beginning there was only water, no land, and everything surrounding it was completely dark. God's Spirit was moving above the water. He said, "Let there be light." And there was light! God looked at what He had done, and He saw that it was good. (You can think of yourself as being like God in that way. When you complete a project that you're proud of and you know it's good, you feel pleased with your work.) God had divided light from darkness. He called the light "day" and the darkness "night." And that was earth's first day ever.

Dear God, daylight is so ordinary that I forget to thank You for creating it. Thank You, God, for light! Amen.

CREATION, DAY TWO

Then God called the open space Heaven.
GENESIS 1:8 NLV

On the first day, there was only water with God's Spirit moving above it. On the second day, God separated the water above the earth from the water below, and then there was sky, the earth's atmosphere, and the air we breathe. God called the open space "heaven." When you look up, you see only part of that open space. You can see clouds, the moon, sun, and stars. But what's beyond that? Scientists have telescopes that have viewed distant stars, but that's as far as we can see into God's creation. The place we think of as heaven is beyond what we can see or even imagine. Heaven is where God and Jesus live. Angels live there too. So do people who have died. Heaven is a real place. We don't know exactly where it is or much about what it looks like. But if we believe in Jesus, we know that heaven will be our home when we die one day. What do you think heaven looks like?

Dear God, thank You for the sky, the air I breathe, and heaven! Amen.

CREATION, DAY THREE

Then God called the dry land Earth.
He called the gathering of the waters Seas.
GENESIS 1:10 NLV

Next, God created the land and the oceans. "Then God said, 'Let plants grow from the earth, plants that have seeds. Let fruit trees grow on the earth that bring their kind of fruit with their own seeds.' And it was so. Plants grew out of the earth, giving their own kind of seeds. Trees grew with their fruit, and their kind of seeds. And God saw that it was good" (Genesis 1:11–12 NLV). At the end of that third day, earth began to look like it does today. There was land, bodies of water like seas and oceans, and all kinds of plants. God gave those plants seeds so that when the seeds were planted there would be even more trees, flowers, vegetables—so many plants! The trees and plants you see today are descendants of what God made on the third day. But God wasn't done yet. Can you think of some things that were missing?

Dear God, thank You for earth and oceans and all kinds of plants! Amen.

CREATION, DAY FOUR

Then God made the two great lights, the brighter light to rule the day, and the smaller light to rule the night. He made the stars also.

GENESIS 1:16 NLV

On the fourth day, God created the sun, moon, and stars. God said, "Let there be lights in the open space of the heavens to divide day from night. Let them tell the days and years and times of the year" (Genesis 1:14 NLV). The sun and moon would be a way for God's people (that hadn't been created yet) to tell time. Each sunrise and sunset would measure one day. God also spoke for the first time about the measurement of time called "years" and also about "times of the year" (seasons). Earth had its land, water, plants, and trees, and now the earth's sky was in place too, with its sun, moon, and stars. Can you imagine what the earth was like on that fourth day? Everything God had made so far was perfect. But there were no animals or people.

Dear God, thank You for the sun, moon, and stars. Thank You for giving us time so we can measure days, years, and seasons. Amen.

STARRY, STARRY NIGHT

He knows the number of the stars. He gives names to all of them.
PSALM 147:4 NLV

Have you been to a backyard movie night or sleepover? It's fun to camp out in the backyard on warm summer nights. Maybe you looked up and saw a falling star, or maybe you looked for the biggest star and made a wish. When you look at the night sky, you are only able to see the stars nearest Earth. But there are many, many stars beyond what you can see. Scientists think there are about two hundred billion trillion stars in the universe, but only God knows for sure. The Bible says God created all the stars. He always knows the exact number of stars in the sky, and He gives names to each one. Two hundred billion trillion stars and each has a name! Did you know that the same God who knows the number of stars also knows the exact number of hairs on your head? It's in the Bible: Matthew 10:30.

Dear God, how great You are to
know how many stars are in the sky.
Thank You, God, for stars. Amen.

Creation, Day Five

God made the big animals that live in the sea,
and every living thing that moves through the waters
by its kind, and every winged bird after its kind.
Genesis 1:21 NLV

A great artist begins painting with one stroke of his brush. He keeps adding details until he is satisfied with his masterpiece and decides it is finished. God is that kind of artist. After He created the earth, He started adding details. Until day five, the only living things were plants. God was ready now to add other living things. First, He created fish and other sea creatures to live in the water. Then God created birds. He said, "Let birds fly above the earth in the open space of the heavens" (Genesis 1:20 NLV). God wanted good to come to these animals. He told them to give birth and increase in number. That was the end of the fifth day. God still wasn't done with His masterpiece. Earth had plants, sea creatures, and birds. Some other living parts were missing. Can you guess what they were?

Dear God, thank You for creating birds and everything that lives in the sea. Amen.

CREATION, DAY SIX

God made man in His own likeness. In the likeness of God He made him. He made both male and female.
GENESIS 1:27 NLV

Day six was a busy day for God as He put the finishing touches on the earth, His masterpiece. The oceans and seas were filled with animals. Birds sang from tree branches and flew through the sky. The land needed animals too. So God made cattle, wild animals, and every kind of animal that moves on the ground. He saw that it was good. There was just one last detail to add, the most important of all. God created a man and a woman. He told them to care for His creation, to care for the plants and to rule over all the animals. He gave the man and woman a beautiful, perfect garden to live in and called it "Eden." God made the man and woman to be somewhat like Him, but not as perfect. God made you to be like Him too. You are a "child of God" just like that first man and woman, Adam and Eve.

Dear God, thank You for creating me to be like You. Amen.

CREATION, DAY SEVEN

Then God honored the seventh day and made it holy, because in it He rested from all His work which He had done.
GENESIS 2:3 NLV

Creating anything takes a lot of time and hard work. What have you created lately? Were you pleased with what you made? When you were finished with your masterpiece, it was time to relax and appreciate what you had done. That's what God did on the seventh day. He rested. In just six days, God had created the heavens and the earth. He made plants, animals, and people. He created a garden for His people to live in, and He set them to work caring for the animals and His earth. God deserved a rest. You deserve a rest too. We set aside Sunday as a day of rest. It's the day when we go to church to honor God and all He does for us. Make Sunday a day when you focus on God, your family, and God's blessings. What are some ways you and your family can relax together?

Dear God, thank You for Sunday and for giving me rest. Amen.

THE GIFT OF FREEDOM

Obey as men who are free but do not use this to cover up sin. Live as servants owned by God at all times.

1 PETER 2:16 NLV

You are a responsible girl. Your parents reward your good behavior by giving you freedom to do most of what you want. But they are still your parents. They have rules they expect you to follow. They expect you to use your freedom wisely and to make good choices. The same was true for Adam and Eve. God gave them freedom to live as they wished. But God ruled the earth and everything else. He made the rules. Adam and Eve had freedom to make their own choices, but they would receive consequences if they broke God's rules. And they did break His rules. They knew they had done wrong, and they were so ashamed that they hid from God. They made excuses for what they had done. So God made them leave their beautiful garden. Freedom is a gift from God. Learn from Adam and Eve to use it wisely. Make good choices and follow the rules.

Dear God, thank You for Your gift of freedom. Amen.

YOU ARE EARTH'S CARETAKER

The earth is the Lord's, and all that is in it,
the world, and all who live in it.
PSALM 24:1 NLV

God gave Adam and Eve the job of caring for the earth. He told them, "Fill the earth and rule over it. Rule over the fish of the sea, over the birds of the sky, and over every living thing that moves on the earth. . . . I have given you every plant that gives seeds. . .and every tree that has fruit. . . . They will be food for you. I have given every green plant for food to every animal of the earth, and to every bird of the sky, and to everything that moves on the earth that has life" (Genesis 1:28–30 NLV). Today you have Adam and Eve's job of caring for God's earth. You can plant a garden, remember to recycle, pick up litter, not waste anything, and reuse whatever you can. What are some other ways you can care for God's earth?

Dear God, I will do my best to help care for the earth and everything in it. Amen.

TEN GREAT LAWS

When the Lord had finished speaking with Moses on Mount Sinai, He gave him the two stone writings of the Law, pieces of stone written on by the finger of God.
EXODUS 31:18 NLV

Adam and Eve were the first humans to disobey God. Their ancestors kept disobeying Him. So God commanded Moses (the leader of God's people, the Israelites) to meet with Him on a mountaintop. When God came down on that mountain, the whole mountain shook. Smoke went up from it, and God was there in a thick cloud. The people saw and were afraid of God's mighty power. On the mountaintop, God gave Moses ten important laws for all to follow. The laws would help everyone know what God expected from them. When God finished speaking to Moses, He gave him two stone tablets. With His own finger, God wrote on them His ten laws. Then Moses went down the mountain and told the people what had happened and what God said. You can find God's ten laws—the Ten Commandments—in the Bible in Exodus 20.

Dear God, thank You for giving us good rules to follow. Amen.

WHO IS NUMBER ONE?

"Have no gods other than Me."
EXODUS 20:3 NLV

Make a short list naming the three most important things in your life. What is first on your list? If you said, "God," good for you! Now, answer this question: How many Gods are there? Did you say, "Just one"? There is only one true God, and the first commandment He gave Moses was "Have no gods other than Me." Anything you make more important than your relationship with the one and only God becomes like a mini god. If things like hanging out with your girlfriends, watching television, playing games, or working at hobbies and sports become more important than your relationship with God, then those are mini gods. Giving those things too much attention can lead you down the wrong path and away from the one true God. Think about it: What are some things you can do to make certain God always comes first in your life?

Dear God, please forgive me for making other things more important than my relationship with You. I want You always to come first. Amen.

BE CAREFUL WHAT YOU WORSHIP

"Do not make for yourselves a god to look like anything that is in heaven above or on the earth below or in the waters under the earth."
EXODUS 20:4 NLV

When Moses came down from the mountain with the Ten Commandments, he discovered that God's people had created a gold statue of a calf. They were worshipping it in the way they had once worshipped God. This upset Moses greatly because God's second commandment was all about not worshipping idols. An idol is something that takes the place of God. It can be a statue, a picture, a real person, or anything else. Moses' friends began to doubt the real God existed, so they created their own fake god, a statue that they prayed to and honored. You can't see God. He is an invisible Spirit, and you need to trust that He exists. You shouldn't treat anything with the same worship and honor that you do God. Be careful what you worship. Making anyone or anything into an idol is wrong.

Dear God, I can't see You,
but I know You exist. I will worship,
pray to, and honor only You. Amen.

GOD'S MAGNIFICENT NAME

"I am the Lord. That is My name. I will not give My shining-greatness to another, or My praise to false gods."
ISAIAH 42:8 NLV

God says, "I am the Lord. That is My name." His name is to be said with respect—always. God's third commandment is "Do not use the name of the Lord your God in a false way" (Exodus 20:7 NLV). Think about how good it feels when someone says your name in a gentle and loving way. How would you feel if someone said your name in an unkind way or made fun of your name? God's name is holy. If you use His name or Jesus' name as a swear word or in any hurtful, angry, or disrespectful way, you dishonor God. It shows others you really don't care about God or respecting Him. Be a girl whose words honor God. Think about it: Do you believe saying "OMG" or "Oh my God" is disrespecting God's name? What could you say instead?

Dear God, Your name is special and more important than any other name, and I will always use Your name with respect. Amen.

SUNDAY

"Remember the Day of Rest, to keep it holy."
EXODUS 20:8 NLV

Weekdays include a mix of work and play. You go to school Monday through Friday. You study, do homework, and help around the house. You do fun activities too, like going to dance class, listening to music, and spending time with your friends. There's no school on the weekend. On Saturday maybe you run errands with your mom or dad, participate in a team sport, or go to a festival or other community event. What about Sunday? Is it different from the rest? God's fourth commandment says to remember that Sunday is a holy day. It is *His* day. It's a day to go to church and learn about and honor God. The Lord commands us to keep Sunday holy by setting aside our work and spending quiet, restful time with family and friends. Sunday is one day of the week we show God how special He is and how much we honor and respect Him.

Dear God, Sunday is about more than just going to church. It's Your special day, and we should spend it thinking about and honoring You. Amen.

GOD'S FIFTH COMMANDMENT

"Honor your father and your mother."
EXODUS 20:12 NLV

You have something in common with those kids who lived way back in Moses' time. When God spoke to Moses on the mountaintop, He said, "Tell the people, 'Honor your father and your mother.'" Even then, God saw kids disrespecting their parents and not following their parents' rules. It must have been very important to God for kids to respect their moms and dads. So important that He made it His fifth commandment. Kids mess up sometimes, even kids like you who are respectful most of the time. When you don't understand the rules your mom and dad make, it can be, well, irritating! You might feel like talking back or pouting or even breaking the rules. But God says, "No!" He wants you to show respect to your mom and dad even when it's hard. Do your best to honor God by also honoring your parents.

Dear God, forgive me for the times I haven't been respectful to my parents. I know they are doing their best to help me grow up. I will try even harder to honor them. Amen.

GOD'S SIXTH COMMANDMENT

*"Blessed are the peacemakers,
for they will be called children of God."*
MATTHEW 5:9 NIV

The Bible tells the true story of a woman named Abigail. She was married to a very rich but mean man named Nabal when he and the future king of Israel (a young warrior, David) became enemies. David and his men had been guarding Nabal's fields and asked Nabal for a favor in return. He wanted Nabal to give him and his men food and supplies. But Nabal said no. David was so angry that he planned to kill Nabal. Abigail bravely went to talk with David. She didn't know how he might react, so she spoke quietly and gently with him. She got David to calm down and change his mind about killing her foolish husband. You can learn an important lesson from Abigail. Be a peacemaker. You might hear about killings in our world, but you can be one to help make a change. Be a peacemaker wherever you go.

Dear God, help me to be wise like Abigail and be someone who brings peace to the world. Amen.

HUSBANDS AND WIVES

Be faithful in marriage.
EXODUS 20:14 CEV

Do you dream of getting married one day? Imagine. There you are in your beautiful wedding dress, standing at the altar with your Prince Charming, promising to love one another forever. Your friends and family are there with big smiles on their faces. Everyone is so happy for you. All wish you a lifetime of loving each other. God's seventh commandment says husbands and wives should be faithful in marriage. That means putting each other ahead of anything or anyone else except God—He should be first in everything. Faithfulness in marriage means giving your partner all your love and respect all the time. It's helping each other and caring for one another, no matter what. God already knows if you will get married, and He knows who you will marry. God knows everything! When you stand at the altar someday with your beloved, you can remember that God is the one who brought the two of you together.

Dear God, You already know my Prince Charming! I wonder who he is and what he's like. I look forward to meeting him. Amen.

WHAT IS STEALING?

"Do not steal."
EXODUS 20:15 NLV

Stealing is taking something without permission that doesn't belong to you. It's also taking something from a store without paying for it. But there are other ways of stealing you might not have thought of. Did you know you can steal time? If your mom was helping your brother with his homework and you kept interrupting because you wanted her attention, that's stealing time that belongs to your brother. You can also steal someone's idea. What if you were talking with a girl in your class about the science project she's making, and her idea sounded so awesome you decided to steal it and make a science project just like hers? Another form of stealing would be spreading lies and gossip. If you say something about someone that isn't true, it's not only hurtful, but it steals that person's reputation—the truth about who she is and what she does. Remember, God says, "Do not steal." So be extra careful you don't take something that belongs to someone else.

Dear God, stealing is hurtful to others and to myself. I promise not to steal. Amen.

A BIG LIE

Do not tell lies about others.

EXODUS 20:16 CEV

The Bible tells about the life of Joseph, the second youngest of several brothers and his dad's favorite. Joseph's dad gave him a fancy coat to wear. Joseph's brothers were jealous, and they made a terrible plan to kill Joseph. One of the brothers, Reuben, convinced the others not to kill Joseph but to trap him in a deep, dry well. (Reuben secretly planned to rescue Joseph later.) The brothers agreed. But before they put Joseph in the well, they stole his coat. Later they dipped it in blood from a dead goat and took the coat to Joseph's dad. "We found this!" they said. Their lie made Joseph's dad think his son was dead. (Read the story in Genesis 37:1–33.) Lying about others is never right. God says so in His ninth commandment. The brothers' lie was a big one, but even telling small lies about others is wrong. Lies can be sneaky. The brothers didn't "find" Joseph's coat. They stole it. Be careful with the words you choose. Always tell the truth.

Dear God, I will obey Your command to be truthful. Amen.

GOD'S TENTH COMMANDMENT

Do not desire to possess anything that belongs to another person.
EXODUS 20:17 CEV

The last of God's Ten Commandments is about jealousy. His people, the Israelites, were on their way to a wonderful place God had promised them. The walk was long and hard. The people were tired and crabby. Maybe God heard them complaining about what rich people had and wanting that for themselves. God says we shouldn't want what others have. That's because God gives us what we need exactly when we need it. His plan is to bless us. We don't always get our blessings right away, but if we are patient, we'll see that God is faithful. He will always keep His promises. Maybe there's a girl at school who wears expensive clothes, or maybe a friend got an expensive gift for Christmas, something you really wanted. Try your hardest not to want what they have. Tell God about it. Ask Him for what you want, and then trust Him to give you what you need.

Dear God, help me to be content with what I have instead of wanting what belongs to others. Amen.

BE YOURSELF

"Have I not told you? Be strong and have strength of heart! Do not be afraid or lose faith. For the Lord your God is with you anywhere you go."

JOSHUA 1:9 NLV

God made you unique—that means special, one of a kind. Sometimes you might feel a little worried that people won't like you just as you are. Maybe someone at school said something negative about what you wore or how you fixed your hair. You decided, wrongly, that it was true. Or maybe you didn't do well on an assignment, and you decided you're not as smart as the other kids. That's not true either! Or maybe you just started at a new school, and you've decided you won't fit in. Again, not true. Don't tell yourself those lies! Don't hide from others who you truly are. God made you. He wants you to be strong and to be proud of the one true you. So let your uniqueness show! You are amazing. Don't be afraid to be yourself.

Dear God, I am special and wonderful just as I am. Help me to show others the one true me. Amen.

SELF-TALK

Do not throw away your trust, for your reward will be great.
HEBREWS 10:35 NLV

It's not only what others say about you that can make you think poorly about yourself, but also what you say to yourself. Maybe your dream is to join a girls' gymnastics team that performs in your local parade. You wonder if you're good enough. You say to yourself, *Those girls all look so good in their costumes. Everything they do is perfect. If I'm not good enough, I might not make the team. What if I fail?* That kind of self-talk can cause you to miss out on many fun things. When you catch yourself saying, *I'm not good enough*, remember that God made you, and He loves you just the way you are. He is the one who gives you confidence and makes you strong. When you learn to trust and believe in His love for you, then you will begin to trust and love yourself.

Dear God, sometimes I talk myself out of doing things because I'm afraid I won't be good at them. You are my helper. Please help me to have more confidence in myself. Amen.

GOD'S GIRL

See what great love the Father has for us
that He would call us His children.
1 JOHN 3:1 NLV

Do you know a girl who got engaged, maybe an older sister, cousin, or close family friend? Were you there when she showed off her engagement ring? When a girl gets engaged, her husband-to-be usually gives her a diamond ring. The diamond is a symbol of his special love for her. Diamonds are precious, valuable stones worthy of appreciation. When a man gives a woman a diamond, it shows that he values and appreciates her. Every diamond is unique, one of a kind. Like snowflakes, no two are exactly alike. They come in different sizes, shapes, and even colors. God made you to be like a diamond. He made you with love, and He wants you to be appreciated. You are of great worth. Like a diamond, there is no one exactly like you. God made you special because you are His child, His girl. He loves you. Remember, you are always worthy of appreciation and respect because you belong to Him.

Dear God, You made me to be respected and loved. Amen.

WORRIES

So we can say for sure, "The Lord is my Helper.
I am not afraid of anything man can do to me."
HEBREWS 13:6 NLV

You lie in bed at night, but you can't sleep because your mind is racing from one thing to another. You have a bad case of the worries. Your thoughts turn to the health of people you love and then to school things like your grades, assignments, and tests. You start to worry about that new thing you have to do, that thing you've never done before, and just thinking about it makes you nervous. A little voice in your head says, *What's going to happen? Will I be safe? Am I ready?* The thoughts keep coming. What's a girl to do? The cure for the worries is faith in God. When you remember that He is your helper, you won't let the worries get you down. If something is worrying you, it's good to talk with someone about it too. God has helpers all around you—parents, teachers, your pastor, and others.

Dear God, I don't have to worry,
because You are my protector.
I am safe when I'm with You. Amen.

TOO MUCH

No temptation has overtaken you except what is common to mankind. And God is faithful; he will not let you be tempted beyond what you can bear. But when you are tempted, he will also provide a way out so that you can endure it.

1 CORINTHIANS 10:13 NIV

Imagine dreaming that your mom told you to put that little pile of dirty clothes on your bedroom floor in the wash. You didn't. The pile started to grow. It grew until it was all around you—stinky socks, sweaty shirts, dirty underwear. Ewww. . . That would be a nightmare! Worries can pile up like dirty laundry. Sometimes they are too much. You might want to scream, "Make it stop!" If that happens, remember everyone has worries. God is with you, helping to make them go away. When they seem like more than you can handle, God will provide you with a way out. Trust Him. Ask for help if those worries are too much. Today they might seem like a lot. But tomorrow is a new day. Things will get better.

Dear God, please lead me out of my worries. Amen.

BRAVE GIRL

I will not be afraid of ten thousands of people
who stand all around against me.
PSALM 3:6 NLV

Because you are God's girl, you have power. Your faith will make you brave. Read Psalm 91 in your Bible. When you put your trust in God, He will be your "safe and strong place" (Psalm 91:2 NLV). You'll be less afraid of any trouble that comes in the night or in the daytime (v. 5). You won't be as afraid of sickness (v. 6). God will protect you like a mother bird protecting her babies under her wings (v. 4). You won't only have God giving you power, but you will have His army of angels protecting you too. The Bible says, "For He will tell His angels to care for you and keep you in all your ways. They will hold you up in their hands" (vv. 11–12 NLV). Thinking about God's army of angels will help you to be brave. Because God loves you, He will get you out of trouble (v. 14). When you call on Him, He will answer you and show you His power (vv. 15–16).

Dear God, thank You for making
me a brave girl. Amen.

First Aid for Fear

When I am afraid, I will trust in You.

Psalm 56:3 nlv

In the Psalms, King David wrote about feeling afraid. He said what he was afraid of, but instead of letting those feelings guide him, David chose to put his trust in God. When you feel afraid, know that God is bigger than your fear. Try this: Make your own fear first aid kit. What should you put inside? Bible verses you've memorized to remind you not to be afraid. You should put people in there too, people you can trust for help. You might add a song or poem you made up to remind you not to be afraid. And you can't have a fear first aid kit without prayer. So put that in there too. David prayed to God, "The troubles of my heart have grown. . . . Look upon my troubles. . . . Keep me safe, Lord, and set me free" (Psalm 25:17–18, 20 nlv). Be like David. Don't allow fear to fill your heart. Trust in God to keep you safe.

Dear God, when I'm afraid, I can run to You for first aid. I will trust in You to keep me safe. Amen.

YOU AREN'T TOO YOUNG!

The LORD said to me, "Do not say, 'I am too young.' You must go to everyone I send you to and say whatever I command you."
JEREMIAH 1:7 NIV

How many times have you heard, "You can't do that because you're too young"? Your age might keep you from doing certain things, but in God's eyes you aren't too young to make a difference. You aren't too young to learn something new. You aren't too young to be helpful and kind or to cheer up people when they feel sad. You're not too young to share what you have with others, to remind people to be more forgiving, or to have hope. You aren't too young to volunteer and to help keep God's earth clean. And don't let anyone say that you're too young to tell others about Jesus. When it comes to doing some of the other things, every day you'll move a little closer to becoming a grown-up. Be patient with God. He will get you there soon enough.

Dear God, I'm never too young to be Your helper. Show me what to do. Amen.

HELP SOMEONE WHO'S SAD

"In every way I showed you that by working hard like this we can help those who are weak."
ACTS 20:35 NLV

Maybe you've been sick with a bad flu bug, and afterward you felt tired and weak for a while. Our bodies sometimes feel weak. But our spirits, our feelings, can feel weak too. A symptom of a weak spirit is sadness. Everyone feels sad sometimes. You can help God comfort those who are sad. If you see that one of your parents, a sibling, or a friend seems a little down, there are things you can do. First, be kind. Be willing to help with little things the person might not feel up to doing. Speak comforting words. Say things like "I'm sorry you're sad," "I love you," "Tell me if I can do anything to help you feel better." You can also help by asking the person if they want to talk about why they're sad. These are all good ways of helping God. Ask God to help with the sadness too.

Dear God, when someone I love is sad, please show me how I can help. Amen.

WHEN I FEEL SAD

The Lord is near to those who have a broken heart.
And He saves those who are broken in spirit.
PSALM 34:18 NLV

When you feel sad, you might wonder whether God sees and hears you when you cry. You might even think God has left you alone. Remember that God is everywhere all the time, so He won't ever leave you. God promises to hear you. He doesn't just hear you when you pray. He hears every word you say. The Bible says that wherever you are—at home in your bedroom, at school, on a playground, at your grandma's house when your family goes to visit, or anywhere—God sees and knows when you cry. He collects your tears in His bottle and writes them down in His book (Psalm 56:8). Think about that the next time you feel sad. God sees your tears. He will comfort you, and He will send His helpers to comfort you too. God understands why you are sad. You can trust Him to help.

Dear God, I'm really hurting. Please help me. Comfort me and send others to help. Amen.

HELP SOMEONE WHO FEELS UNLOVED

"This is what I tell you to do:
Love each other just as I have loved you."
JOHN 15:12 NLV

Ask God to help you look around and notice people who feel unloved. If there's a really quiet girl in your class who has no friends, she might feel unloved. What about the old lady who lives across the street? No one ever comes to visit her. Maybe she feels unloved. The homeless people in your community, those you see lined up waiting for food at the shelter—they might feel unloved too. You aren't too young to help. Make friends with that quiet girl. Ask your girlfriends to welcome her too. Invite her to hang out with you. Bake some cookies for the lady across the street. Visit with her. Ask your parents if they'll invite her over for dinner. Find out about ways you can help the homeless in your community. Be God's helper and spread His love around.

Dear God, please open my eyes to see these people who feel unloved. Show me how I can help. Use me to spread Your love to others. Amen.

DOES GOD REALLY LOVE ME?

For I know that nothing can keep us from the love of God. Death cannot! Life cannot! Angels cannot! Leaders cannot! Any other power cannot! Hard things now or in the future cannot! The world above or the world below cannot! Any other living thing cannot keep us away from the love of God.

Romans 8:38–39 NLV

If you doubt whether God loves you, think about this: God spends all His time with you. He promises never to leave you. God loves you so much that He hears every word you say and He sees everything you do. God listens and watches because He cares for you. He wants to help you if any trouble comes your way, and He wants to guide you away from sin. God made you. He cares so much about you that He always knows everything going on with you, even how many hairs are on your head! He counts your tears, and He comforts you. God loves you today, and He will love you forever.

Dear God, if anything tries to keep me from believing in Your love, guide me back to You. Amen.

HELP OTHERS GROW THEIR FAITH

Christian brothers, be careful that not one of you has a heart so bad that it will not believe and will turn away from the living God. Help each other.

HEBREWS 3:12–13 NLV

You've been learning so much about God, and your faith in Him is growing every day. You can help your friends and family members grow their faith too. The best way is to be like Jesus as best you can in the ways you talk and act. Then others will see Him through you. If someone thanks you for helping or being kind, you can say, "I'm just doing what Jesus would do." You can encourage those who are sad or troubled by telling them, "God will help you." When you bring Jesus' and God's names into your conversations with others, it might lead to them wanting to know more. When you share your faith through actions and words, you are one of Jesus' ambassadors, helping the whole world to know about Him.

Dear God, please help me lead others to You. I want everyone to know about You and have faith in You. Amen.

WHEN SOMEONE IS TIRED

Moses' hands became tired. So they took a stone and put it under him, and he sat on it. Then Aaron and Hur held up his hands, one on each side. His hands did not move until the sun went down.

EXODUS 17:12 NLV

God's people, the Israelites, were in a battle with an enemy army. The Israelites' leader, Moses, held a stick in his hands. As long as he raised his hands upward, God's power came down and the Israelites' army was winning the battle. But after a while, Moses' arms became tired. When he couldn't hold up his hands any longer, the enemy army started to win. Moses' brother, Aaron, and a friend, Hur, rushed in to help. They made a place for Moses to sit, and then they held up Moses' arms so he could rest. Everyone gets tired sometimes and needs help. When you see that others are tired, you can help by doing some of the hard work for them. If your mom felt tired, what could you do to help her?

Dear God, when I notice that someone is tired, please show me what I can do to help. Amen.

ALL WORN OUT

I will lie down and sleep in peace. O Lord, You alone keep me safe.

PSALM 4:8 NLV

When God formed your body, He knew it would sometimes need to rest. He gave your body the ability to go to sleep for a while so it can prepare for the next day. Everyone needs sleep, but kids especially need it. A good night's rest will help your brain to think better so you can pay attention to your teachers and do well in school. Sleep also helps with your attitude. If you're tired all the time, you will be cranky and not so much fun to be around. Getting enough rest can also help your body fight off germs that get inside. So when bedtime comes, you might want to stay up later, but remember that God wants you to go to sleep. You could think of it as His gift to you—a mini vacation in Dreamland. When you cuddle up cozy under the blankets, you can rest in peace, knowing that God is there keeping you safe while you rest.

Dear God, thank You for Your gift of sleep. Amen.

HELP SOMEONE FIND HOPE

Help each other in troubles and problems.
This is the kind of law Christ asks us to obey.
GALATIANS 6:2 NLV

Imagine that you and your girlfriends have decided to enter a talent show at your church. You discuss what you might do, and you decide to make up a dance to perform. But when you begin practicing, one of your friends keeps messing up the steps. Finally, she sits down on the floor and starts to cry. "It's hopeless!" she says. "I'm not a good dancer." God wants us to help one another with our troubles. You can be a helper by giving others hope when they want to give up. What could you do to help your friend? You could remind her that everyone has trouble learning new things. Then you could patiently help her to learn each of the dance steps one by one. When you help others to have hope that they can accomplish something, you are also helping them to feel good about themselves.

Dear God, when others want to give up, guide me to be the one who gives them hope. Amen.

I WILL HOPE IN THE LORD

For the Lord is a God of what is right and fair.
And good will come to all those who hope in Him.
ISAIAH 30:18 NLV

Hope means expecting something to happen or expecting something to be true. You hope you will win the spelling contest. You hope it won't rain while you're at sleepover camp. Hoping in the Lord is a little different. It means you expect God to be everything He says He is and to do everything He promises to do. Hope goes hand in hand with patience. You must wait to find out if what you hope for will happen. Even if you don't get what you hope for—winning the contest, no rain at sleepover camp—you can continue to put all your hope in God, expecting that He still loves you, takes care of you, keeps His promises, and answers your prayers in ways that are best for you. Hope is about having a good attitude too. It's expecting God to give you something good and not giving up if it doesn't happen right away.

Dear God, teach me to put all
my hope in You. Amen.

IT'S ALL ABOUT ATTITUDE

Christian brothers, keep your minds thinking about whatever is true, whatever is respected, whatever is right, whatever is pure, whatever can be loved, and whatever is well thought of. If there is anything good and worth giving thanks for, think about these things.

PHILIPPIANS 4:8 NLV

Your attitude is the way you think or feel about something or someone. You can have a good attitude or an attitude that is grumpy, angry, and complaining. A good attitude is hopeful. It looks on the bright side of things. Even on bad days, a good attitude has hope that things will get better. Jesus' follower Paul wrote about what makes a good attitude. He said it's thinking about things that are true, respected, right, and pure. He said it's thinking about what's loved and the good things about others. A good attitude remembers to be thankful, and especially thankful to God for His loving-kindness. Check your attitude today. Is it good? If not, ask God to help you turn it around.

Dear God, please help me to have a good attitude, to always have hope, and to be thankful. Amen.

IS IT TRUE?

Think about these things and the Lord will help you understand them.

2 TIMOTHY 2:7 NLV

Paul said you should keep your mind thinking about what is true. How do you know if something is true? Sometimes it's really easy because of what you already know. If someone told you that he had traveled to a planet in a galaxy far away, you would know that wasn't true because you have the facts about how far humans have traveled into space. Sometimes, though, it's more difficult to tell truth from lies. If you are unsure, you can test what you think is true. Does it sound like something God would say? Does it match up with things you've read in the Bible? Does it feel right? God speaks to you in your heart. If something doesn't seem right, He will lead you away from it. If you are unsure if something is true, you can ask someone older and wiser, a parent, teacher, or other grown-up. And always talk with God when you are unsure. He will help you to understand.

Dear God, when I am unsure about something, guide me to the truth. Amen.

IS IT RESPECTFUL?

The one who shows respect is always greater than the one who receives it.
HEBREWS 7:7 NLV

Respect is caring about how your words and actions affect others. If your sister let you borrow her tablet and you left it out in the rain, you would be disrespecting her trust in you and also what belongs to her. Respect comes in many forms. It is being polite even when you don't feel like it and obeying the rules even when you don't like them. It is being careful not to harm or damage what belongs to others, and that includes God's earth and His animals. When you are out in public, respect means watching your manners and not acting up. It's being quiet when your siblings are doing their homework or when your mom or dad is trying to sleep. Think about other ways to be respectful. God sees when you show respect, and it pleases Him. You are becoming even better at being a kind and caring girl.

Dear God, please open my eyes to all the ways I can show respect to people, places, and things. Amen.

THINK OF WHAT'S RIGHT

Sinful men do not understand what is right and fair, but those who look to the Lord understand all things.

PROVERBS 28:5 NLV

Not everyone reads the Bible. They don't know what God says is right and wrong. But you do! You've been learning God's rules and doing your best to follow them. The Bible says we should think about what is right. It's important to think about it all day long. Why? Because you might be around people who don't know God. They don't know right from wrong, and sometimes they might try to lead you to doing what isn't right or fair. Jesus' follower Paul sent a letter to his friend Timothy. Paul wrote, "May your heart always say you are right. Some people have not listened to what their hearts say. They have done what they knew was wrong. Because of this, their faith in Christ was wrecked" (1 Timothy 1:19 NLV). Be careful when you think about what is right and wrong. Listen to your heart.

Dear God, keep my thoughts centered on whether something is right or wrong, and help me to do what is right. Amen.

PURE IN HEART

"Blessed are the pure in heart, for they will see God."
MATTHEW 5:8 NIV

Jesus' follower Paul wrote a letter to his church friends. He reminded them to think about things that are pure and pleasing to God. Being pure means to be careful about what you watch, read, listen to, and do. If you watch a movie that has violence, swear words, and characters doing what God wouldn't approve of, that movie might lead your thoughts away from what's pure and good. The same is true about what you read. Do the characters' words and actions in the stories and books you read lead your thoughts from what is right to what's wrong? In the end, do the characters turn away from what's wrong? What about the words in the songs you listen to? Are those words God approved? You should also think carefully about what you do so you will make decisions that are pleasing to God. Pure thoughts are good thoughts, thoughts that God would approve of.

Dear God, help me to be careful of what I allow into my thoughts, eyes, ears, and heart. Amen.

THINGS I LOVE

We have come to know and believe the love God has for us. God is love.
1 JOHN 4:16 NLV

Have a contest with family members or friends to see who can make the longest list of things they love. Your list may include objects (toys, things you eat, things you wear, etc.), people you love (parents, siblings, friends, etc.), places you love (gardens, zoos, school, etc.), things you love to do (dance, listen to music, play games, etc.), things you love to see (rainbows, sunsets, art, etc.), and things that make you feel loved (hugs, special treats, getting tucked in at night, etc.). You can set a time limit on your contest, or you can keep adding to your list until someone runs out of ideas. You will discover that God gives you many things to love. That's because God *is* love. Think about that. Everything God does and all the blessings you have are because God loves you.

Dear God, help me to think of everything I love and to remember that it all comes from You. Amen.

SPREAD SOME LOVE AROUND

Dear friends, let us love each other, because love comes from God. Those who love are God's children and they know God.
1 JOHN 4:7 NLV

Paul said it's good to keep our minds thinking about whatever can be loved. You've been thinking about things you love, people you love, places you love, things you love to do and see, and what makes you feel loved. Now it's time to give some thought to how you can spread some love around. You could make something for someone, draw a picture, or bake a yummy treat to share. You could write a little love note or make a card. You could give your mom a big hug when she's feeling stressed. You could show some extra love for your pet by brushing its fur, playing with it, or just letting it rest quietly when it wants to. You could show God's earth some love by raking leaves, planting flowers, or picking up trash. These are just a few things you could do to spread some love around. Can you think of others?

Dear God, show me different ways I can spread some love. Amen.

WELL THOUGHT OF

"I am pleased to tell you about the wonderful things which the Most High God has done for me."
DANIEL 4:2 NLV

Paul said we should think about things that are well thought of. It means we should think about what God says is good. Do you think having respect for others is well thought of? God is pleased when you show respect for your parents, teachers, friends, and even strangers. God is pleased when you see the good in people. He says it's good to be forgiving, caring, and loving. It's good to think about treating others with fairness. It's good to think about being helpful and to put those helpful thoughts into action. Think about how Jesus acted toward others. Then try to think more like Him. When you think about whatever is well thought of by God, it will lead you closer to Him.

Dear God, help me to think more like You do. Show me what You think well of. Then help me to put my thoughts into action. I not only want to think more like You; I want to be more like You. Amen.

THANKFUL

Everything God made is good. We should not put anything aside if we can take it and thank God for it.

1 TIMOTHY 4:4 NLV

The list Paul made of what we should think about is worth remembering. He said to think about whatever is true, respected, right, and pure. Think about whatever can be loved and whatever is well thought of. That's a lot to think about, isn't it? Paul ended his list by saying, "If there is anything good and worth giving thanks for, think about these things" (Philippians 4:8 NLV). It's time for you to make a list. Think about and jot down everything you are thankful for. Keep the list by your bed, and when you pray each night, start by thanking God for something on your list. It's always good to begin your prayers by thanking God. When you do that, you're remembering to put Him first. Thank God, tell Him how wonderful you think He is, and then talk with Him about what you want and need.

Dear God, I have so many good things to be thankful for, and all of them are because of You. Thank You, God! Amen.

THANKFUL ALL THE TIME

Give thanks whatever happens. That is what God wants for you in Christ Jesus.

1 THESSALONIANS 5:18 NCV

"Give thanks whatever happens." Sometimes what God asks us to do is hard. How can you be thankful when things aren't going your way? The Bible tells us that Paul was traveling on a wooden ship during a huge windstorm. All the men on the ship were terrified. The ship was about to break apart, and they worried they would die. Paul had faith they would be okay because God's angel had come to Paul and told him so. Paul recognized that the men had been so busy trying to save the ship that they hadn't eaten. They needed to eat to keep up their strength. So Paul got some bread and thanked God for it, and all the men ate. In the middle of that terrible storm, Paul found something to thank God for. That's what God wants us to do. No matter how bad things get, we can always find something to be thankful for.

Dear God, please teach me to be thankful all the time, not just when things are going my way. Amen.

A LOYAL FRIEND

Many will say they are loyal friends,
but who can find one who is truly reliable?
PROVERBS 20:6 NLT

Do you have a loyal friend, someone you can trust all the time? A loyal friend will never let you down. She will always keep the promises she makes to you. Ruth, in the Bible, was that kind of friend. Ruth and her mother-in-law, Naomi, were going through a very hard time. Both of their husbands had died, and they were alone. Naomi thanked Ruth for being such a good daughter-in-law. She told Ruth to leave her and go be with her family members who lived a long distance away. But Ruth refused to leave Naomi. She said, "Don't ask me to leave you and turn back. Wherever you go, I will go; wherever you live, I will live" (Ruth 1:16 NLT). Ruth was a loyal and loving friend. Think about your friends. Can you trust them to stay with you no matter what?

Dear God, thank You for giving me loyal friends I can trust. Help me to be the kind of friend who can be trusted and reliable all the time. Amen.

THE MOST LOYAL OF ALL

"Know then that the Lord your God is God, the faithful God. He keeps His promise and shows His loving-kindness to those who love Him and keep His Laws, even to a thousand family groups in the future."
DEUTERONOMY 7:9 NLV

In your lifetime you will have many friends. Some will be lifelong friends, loyal friends who stick with you through good times and bad. You will never have a friend, though, who is more loyal than God. When you make Him your best friend, He will never leave you. He will keep His promises and show loving-kindness to you forever. And here is where God's friendship and loyalty is different from all others—His promises go on forever. Maybe your parents have taught you about God and His promises. Someday you will pass along to your children what you know about God and His faithfulness, and they will tell their kids, who will tell their kids. . .and on and on. God's loyal friendship goes on forever.

Dear God, You are the best friend I will ever have. Thank You for promising to stay with me forever. Amen.

WISDOM

She opens her mouth with wisdom.
The teaching of kindness is on her tongue.
PROVERBS 31:26 NLV

Who is the wisest person you know? Maybe it's your mom or your dad. They know a lot about life, and they are always ready to share their wisdom with you. They teach you with kindness to be wise about your safety, the friends you choose, and the decisions you make. But God is the wisest one of all. Wisdom comes from Him. The Bible talks about His loving-kindness. Because God loves you, He sets rules for you to follow. The Bible, His instruction book, is filled with God's wisdom. It teaches you what God says is right and wrong. If you follow God's instructions, then you will become wise. The Bible tells about a king named Solomon. God said to Solomon, "Ask Me for anything and I will give it to you" (2 Chronicles 1:7 NLV). Solomon asked God for wisdom, and God gave Solomon what he asked for. Solomon became very wise. He wrote a whole book for the Bible in which he shared his wisdom.

Dear God, give me some of Your wisdom.
Help me to become wise. Amen.

SOLOMON SAYS

These are the wise sayings of Solomon, son of David, king of Israel: They show you how to know wisdom and teaching, to find the words of understanding. . . . They give wisdom to the child-like, and much learning and wisdom to those who are young.

PROVERBS 1:1–2, 4 NLV

King Solomon wrote the Bible book called Proverbs. A proverb is a short saying that includes a wise thought. Not all proverbs come from Solomon. You might have heard some of the others: "An apple a day keeps the doctor away." "You can't judge a book by its cover." "The early bird catches the worm." People made those up; still, they include wise advice. Solomon's proverbs are a bit different because they come from God. They are short sayings that teach us how God wants us to live. Sometimes Solomon used insects and animals to create picture stories for our minds. Those picture stories make us think. As we learn to understand them, we grow in wisdom.

Dear God, I would like to know more about what Solomon has to say. Help me, please, to understand his proverbs. Amen.

BEAUTY OR WISDOM?

A beautiful woman who does not think well is like a gold ring in the nose of a pig.
PROVERBS 11:22 NLV

Solomon painted a picture with this proverb. Can you see that pig in your mind? Do you see her grunting and rolling on the ground, happily covering herself in mud while wearing a lovely gold ring? That's a silly picture, isn't it? But how does a beautiful woman fit into Solomon's story? That's the part Solomon wants you to think about. His story is an example of how a wise woman should behave. If she gets all dressed up to go out but then isn't wise about her behavior, people won't notice her beauty. Her beauty won't be what others see first. Instead, they will notice that she's behaving badly. Solomon's stories remind you to think about things. Wonder and ask questions. What you learn will make you wise.

Dear God, remind me to think and ask questions. Show me what You want me to learn. Amen.

ANTS

"Ants are creatures of little strength,
yet they store up their food in the summer."
PROVERBS 30:25 NIV

Solomon wrote in his book, "Ants—they aren't strong, but they store up food all summer" (Proverbs 30:25 NLT). Think about that. What do you know about ants? You know ants are tiny. You might miss seeing one unless you are looking for it. One ant isn't very strong. A blast of water from a garden hose can send it catapulting through the air. You might not notice a single ant, but you will notice ants when they show up in large numbers. When you see a bunch of them all together, hauling tiny bits of food to their anthill, they get your attention. What do you suppose Solomon's proverb means? What advice does it give you? By itself, one ant is able to accomplish just a little. But by working together, ants accomplish a lot. If you had a ton of food to store, would it be wise to ask for help? A group of helpers is stronger than just one.

Dear God, help me to remember to watch animals and see what I can learn from them. Amen.

THERE'S A LION IN THE WAY!

The lazy man says, "There is a lion outside!
I will be killed in the streets!"
PROVERBS 22:13 NLV

Are you ready for another of Solomon's proverbs? Picture this in your mind. What if it was time for your dad to get up for work tomorrow and he decided he'd rather not go. You find him sitting at the breakfast table still in his pajamas. "Dad, aren't you going to work today?" you ask. He says, "No! There's a lion in the way! There's a lion in the streets!" That would be enough to send you rushing to look out the window, wouldn't it? But you wouldn't see a lion. Your dad made up an excuse because he didn't want to go to work. Solomon's lion story in Proverbs 22:13 is a reminder that lazy people often make up excuses so they don't have to do what needs to get done. Of course, your dad isn't lazy. It's just a made-up story. But Solomon reminds you that laziness isn't wise.

Dear God, Solomon gives good advice.
I will read more of his proverbs
and learn from them. Amen.

TWO HOUSES

Be careful how you live. Live as men who are wise and not foolish.
EPHESIANS 5:15 NLV

Like Solomon, Jesus told little stories with lessons. His stories are called "parables." Think about this parable Jesus told: "Anyone who hears and obeys these teachings of mine is like a wise person who built a house on solid rock. Rain poured down, rivers flooded, and winds beat against that house. But it was built on solid rock, and so it did not fall. Anyone who hears my teachings and doesn't obey them is like a foolish person who built a house on sand. Rain poured down, rivers flooded, and the winds blew and beat against that house. Finally, it fell with a crash" (Matthew 7:24–27 CEV). Did you imagine the house built on rock still standing after the storm? Jesus was speaking about having strong faith in His teachings. When our faith in Him is strong, we're like that house. Nothing can destroy us. When faith is weak, we're like that house built on sand that was swept away.

Dear Jesus, You are the best teacher. Help me to build up my faith in You. Amen.

THE LOST SHEEP

"I am the Good Shepherd. I know My sheep and My sheep know Me."
JOHN 10:14 NLV

Imagine this parable as a picture story: "What would you do if you had 100 sheep and one of them wandered off? Wouldn't you leave the 99 on the hillside and go look for the one that had wandered away? I am sure that finding it would make you happier than having the 99 that never wandered off" (Matthew 18:12–13 CEV). Think about Jesus' story. Ninety-nine sheep followed the shepherd and stayed with him, but one ran off. The shepherd hurried to find it and bring it home. Jesus' story reminds us that He is the good shepherd. We are His sheep. He wants us to live right by following Him. But if some people leave Him to do what's wrong, He will look for them so He can lead them back home. If you get lost, Jesus will never stop looking for you. He loves you and wants you to be with Him.

Dear Jesus, I love You too. If I ever run away from You, hurry to find me and bring me home. Amen.

I NEED SOME SPACE!

Jesus had His followers get into the boat. He told them to go ahead of Him. . .while He sent the people away. After He had sent them away, He went up the mountain by Himself to pray.
MATTHEW 14:22–23 NLV

You've had a busy day at school. When you get home, all you want is some quiet time alone. But your siblings are being noisy, your mom wants you to help with supper, Dad is reminding you that homework has to get done before you watch TV, and the dog is begging you for a walk. Finally, you've had enough. You shout, "I just need some space!" Everyone feels like you do. Sometimes we all need space to be alone and rest. Jesus felt that way too. After He gave an important speech to thousands of people, He wanted to rest and pray. So Jesus sent His followers away. It's okay to ask for space when you need it. But instead of shouting, "I need space!" try saying it in a kinder, gentler way.

Dear Jesus, will You come and rest with me for a while? Amen.

A TIME FOR EVERYTHING

There is a special time for everything. There is a time for everything that happens under heaven.
ECCLESIASTES 3:1 NLV

What if when you woke up this morning you discovered that time had gotten all mixed up? What if morning had turned into night? Instead of it being time for you to get up, time had flip-flopped. It's time to get ready for bed. When you went to bed last night, you opened your window to let in the warm summer breeze. But now you feel cold—really cold! You decide to close the window, and when you do, in the moonlight you see snow covering the ground. Wait. What? It's supposed to be summer! Even the seasons aren't happening at the right times. What if there wasn't a special time for everything, and time just kept changing? From one day to the next, you wouldn't know what was going to happen. That would be confusing and scary, wouldn't it? When God created the earth, He created time as a part of His plan. The Bible says God made a special time for everything.

Dear God, thank You for Your gift of time. Amen.

SEASONS

There is a time to be born, and a time to die;
a time to plant, and a time to pick what is planted.
ECCLESIASTES 3:2 NLV

Spring—the earth is stirring. Leaves appear on branches, hibernating animals wake up and leave their dens, and birds sing louder and more often. In springtime, farmers plant seeds. When summertime comes, those seeds become strong green plants. Summer brings warm weather, sunshine, and fun. The farmer harvests his crops, and then autumn arrives. Leaves fall from branches, animals store food for winter, and sweaters get traded for jackets and coats. Winter comes. The trees are bare again; animals are hibernating. The earth is asleep. The Bible says everything has its season. God created everything to go through a cycle. Things live and die. The same is true for people. For those who know Jesus, when their bodies die their souls live on in heaven with Him. They have eternal life. That means their lives will go on forever.

Dear God, I thank You that when my earthly body dies, everything else that is me will live on with You in heaven. Amen.

DO-OVERS

There is. . .a time to break down, and a time to build up.
ECCLESIASTES 3:3 NLV

Imagine yourself as a crafty girl who loves making beaded jewelry. You gather all your materials and begin crafting. But after you've worked awhile, you look at what you've created and decide it's not quite right. You break down what you've done, remove all the beads, and start over. Or imagine you are in a play and help build the set. When the play is over, you help take it down. Look around you. You'll see all kinds of things being built up or taken down. Do-overs are a part of life. The Bible says there is a time for do-overs, a time to build up and a time to break down. God gives His people a special kind of do-over. When we mess up and allow sin to creep into our lives, God forgives us. He allows us more chances to do over. God says we can break down our mistakes and try again as if the mistakes never happened.

Dear God, thank You for do-overs.
Thank You for Your gift of forgiveness. Amen.

A TIME TO DANCE

There is a time to cry, and a time to laugh;
a time to have sorrow, and a time to dance.
ECCLESIASTES 3:4 NLV

Like everything else, feelings come and go. This morning you could have been excited about the soccer game you had this afternoon. When you got to the field, you practiced, hung out with your teammates, had fun, and laughed. During the game, your team was winning, and that made you happy. Your happiness was dashed, though, when the other team scored the winning goal. On the ride home, you felt disappointed and sad. Every day we have many different feelings. What's important is what we do with them. When we remember that God loves us and is always on our side, feelings like disappointment and sadness don't last as long. The Bible says, "Crying may last for a night, but joy comes with the new day" (Psalm 30:5 NLV). God will turn your sadness around. You will be happy again—maybe even happy enough to dance.

Dear God, thank You for loving me through my sad feelings and helping me to be happy again. Amen.

TO KEEP OR NOT TO KEEP

There is. . .a time to keep, and a time to throw away.
ECCLESIASTES 3:6 NLV

Your room, drawers, bookcases, and closet are packed with stuff. Your mom says it's time to decide what to keep and what to throw away. As you go through your things, some are easy to let go of. Some you know you want to keep. Those decisions aren't hard. But what about the stuff you're unsure of? You have to think about that for a while. God wants you to think about everything you allow into your life, not just your stuff. Think about what kinds of behavior are worth keeping and which you should throw away. Anything that pleases God and leads you nearer to Him is good to keep. Anything that displeases Him you should get rid of—things like bad habits, naughty language, lying, bullying, and being disrespectful. Can you think of others? Can you think of some good ways of behaving that you should hang on to?

Dear God, help me to sort through the ways I behave and keep only what's good. Amen.

A TIME TO SPEAK

There is. . .a time to be quiet, and a time to speak.
ECCLESIASTES 3:7 NLV

Good for you! You're becoming wiser. You think more often now about what is pleasing to God and what isn't. You make better choices because you want to please Him. And you've also discovered there's a right time for everything, including the ways you behave. What about being quiet—is there a right time for that? Most often it's easy to know when it's best not to speak up. But sometimes you might be unsure. What if a friend told you a secret about someone and it worried you? That would be a time to speak up and share what you know with a parent or other trusted adult. If you saw a friend about to do something dangerous, that would be a good time to speak up too. What if you saw a classmate being made fun of? Would that be a good time to say something? Ask God to help you decide when to be silent and when to speak up.

Dear God, guide me to know when quiet is good and when it's best to speak. Amen.

WHAT IS COMPASSION?

Last of all, you must share the same thoughts and the same feelings. Love each other with a kind heart and with a mind that has no pride.

1 PETER 3:8 NLV

Compassion is a big and a very important word. It means truly caring about and understanding how others feel. If you saw someone crying, you could understand how that person feels because you have felt sad and cried. If you saw someone get angry, you could understand that feeling because you've felt angry sometimes. The Bible says we should have compassion for others—we should share their feelings. It tells us something else: to love others with a kind heart. If you were a girl without compassion, you might think you are better than others. But you are a compassionate girl! Compassion comes from understanding that you are just like everyone else. You have the same feelings and many of the same thoughts. How could you show some love and kindness to a person who is angry or sad?

Dear God, please open my eyes and ears to the feelings others have, and help me to have compassion. Amen.

COMPASSION IN ACTION

"He went up to the man. As he saw him, he had loving-pity on him."
LUKE 10:33 NLV

Jesus told a story about a man who was robbed and beaten. He was hurt badly and left to die in the street. A man passing by saw the person lying there, but instead of asking if he could help, the man crossed the street and walked on the other side. A second man came along. He came nearer to the injured person, but then he decided to keep going. Before long, a third man arrived. When he saw someone was hurt, he went right up to him. He had compassion for the man. He cared for him and got him help. He didn't leave until he knew the person would be all right. Jesus asked His followers, "Which of these three do you think was a neighbor to the man who was beaten?" (Luke 10:36 NLV). Can you answer Jesus' question? What would you do if you saw someone in trouble?

Dear God, if I see someone hurt or in trouble, I will do my best to help. Amen.

BE SAFE

Good thinking will keep you safe. Understanding will watch over you.

PROVERBS 2:11 NLV

You are a girl who wants to help others. If you see someone in trouble, you want to rush right in and do something. It's good to help, but be careful you don't put yourself in danger too. Sometimes, as much as you want to help, you can't do it alone. Wise Solomon wrote in Proverbs, "Good thinking will keep you safe." Think about this: If you saw a baby duck had fallen deep down in a crevice among some rocks, would you climb in alone and try to save it? What if you both got stuck? There's a saying that isn't from the Bible, but still, it's good advice: "Look before you leap." It means think! Before you rush in alone to help, think if it would be better to get help. Say a quick prayer and ask God what you should do. He is always with you. You can trust Him to guide you in the right direction.

Dear God, help me to know when it's wise to help by myself and when I need a buddy. Amen.

TWO SISTERS

*"Only a few things are important,
even just one. Mary has chosen the good
thing. It will not be taken away from her."*
LUKE 10:42 NLV

Jesus was at the home of His friends, two sisters named Mary and Martha. While Martha was working hard getting supper ready for their guests, Mary sat with Jesus, listening to His every word. This upset Martha. Finally, she'd had enough. She said to Jesus, "Do You see that my sister is not helping me? Tell her to help me." Jesus answered, "Martha, Martha, you are worried and troubled about many things. Only a few things are important, even just one. Mary has chosen the good thing. It will not be taken away from her" (Luke 10:40–42 NLV). Jesus reminded Martha that paying attention to Him was more important than anything else she had to do. How are you at giving all your attention to Jesus? Would you rather do other things than read the Bible, pray, and learn more about Him?

Dear Jesus, forgive me for not giving You my attention. Spending time with You is more important than anything else. Amen.

KEEP DOING WHAT'S RIGHT

Keep your heart telling you that you have done what is right. If men speak against you, they will be ashamed when they see the good way you have lived as a Christian.

1 PETER 3:16 NLV

Sometimes it's not easy being a Jesus follower. Jesus' disciples found that out after Jesus died, arose from being dead, and went back up to heaven. The disciples tried to share the good news about Jesus, but everywhere they went, they found some people who didn't believe. They made fun of the disciples. When you talk about Jesus with others, some might not believe. Some may even make fun of you. But don't let that stop you. Following Jesus, talking about Him, and obeying His rules are all the right thing to do. When you follow Jesus, you are setting a good example for others. Maybe God will open their eyes to see that, and they might become Jesus' followers too.

Dear Jesus, I will keep following You, talking about You, and obeying You. If others make fun of me because they don't agree, I won't let that get in my way. Amen.

GOD OR SON OF GOD?

"My Father and I are one!"
JOHN 10:30 NLV

Jesus is God's Son, but He is also God. How can that be? God has the incredible power to be three persons in one. He is the Father, Creator and ruler of everything. We only know the part of God's creation we see. We wonder what exists beyond it. Jesus is another part of God. The Bible says Jesus has existed with God forever. He was in heaven with God before He came down to earth as a baby. There's a third part of God, the Holy Spirit. He's the part who speaks to your heart and guides you to do what's right. There's so much about God that's a mystery. It's hard to understand how God is three persons in one. But it's easier to understand if we think of those parts separately. We can't see God, so we use our faith to believe in Him and all that He is. We only know what the Bible tells us.

Dear God, there's so much about You we can't understand. We will never be as smart as You or as perfect. Amen.

HE IS RISEN!

"He is not here. He is risen."

LUKE 24:6 NLV

Jesus did many amazing things while He was here on earth, but nothing was more amazing than the reason God sent Him here. Jesus' purpose was to show us that sin leads to dying, but it doesn't have to be that way if we trust in His death as the punishment for our sin. There's no place in heaven for sin. When Jesus died on the cross, He made a way for all our sin to be forgiven. Men put Jesus' body inside a tomb. But three days later, Jesus came back from death, body and all! It was God's way of showing us that we can live again after we die. If we ask God to forgive our sins and we believe in Jesus' death and resurrection, we can live forever in heaven. God's plan is for us to believe in His Son, Jesus.

Dear God, thank You for sending us Jesus and making a way for me to be with You in heaven someday. Amen.

SAVIOR—WITH A CAPITAL S

"We know that this man really is the Savior of the world."
JOHN 4:42 NIV

Another name for Jesus is Savior. A savior is someone who saves a person from harm. For example, a lifeguard who saves a person from drowning can be called a savior. But notice that word *savior* begins with a lowercase *s*. We use an uppercase *S* when we talk about Jesus as Savior because He is the most important Savior of all. Jesus saved us from being punished for our sins. Before Jesus came, people made sacrifices to God as a way of seeking forgiveness so God wouldn't punish them. These ancient people owned herds of cattle and sheep. Animals were valuable and sold or traded for money. Often people would give the best and most valuable lamb from their flock to God as a sacrifice. When Jesus died on the cross, He sacrificed His life for us. He gave up His life to save us from ever being punished for our sins. That is why Jesus is the most wonderful Savior of all. He is the Savior of the world.

Dear Jesus, thank You for being my Savior. Amen.

THE HOLY SPIRIT

"The Helper is the Holy Spirit. The Father will send Him in My place. He will teach you everything and help you remember everything I have told you."
JOHN 14:26 NLV

The Holy Spirit is the part of God that lives inside your heart. He speaks to you and reminds you about right and wrong. The Holy Spirit is your helper. He helps you to be brave when you are scared. He gives you strength to keep going when you want to give up. He is sometimes known as the Comforter because He helps you to feel better when you're sad. God's Holy Spirit puts love, joy, peace, patience, kindness, goodness, faithfulness, gentleness, and self-control inside your heart (Galatians 5:22–23). He will help you understand what you read in the Bible. He even prays in your place when you don't know what to say. You can always count on the Holy Spirit to live in your heart because He is a part of God—and God promises never to leave you.

Dear God, thank You for the part of You that is the Holy Spirit. I feel You each day living inside my heart. Amen.

FRUIT OF THE SPIRIT

It will be this way until the Spirit is poured out upon us from heaven, and the desert becomes a field giving so much fruit, that it seems as if it has many trees.
ISAIAH 32:15 NLV

Have you seen pictures of deserts that have nothing but sand? Deserts like that are called "wastelands." Without God's Holy Spirit living inside you, your heart would be like a desert where there is nothing. But when God comes and lives in your heart, He plants good "seeds" in there, and they begin to grow. The Bible calls them "the fruit of the Spirit." When the Holy Spirit lives in your heart, the seeds He plants help you to grow in "love, joy, peace, not giving up, being kind, being good, having faith, being gentle, and being the boss over [your] own desires" (Galatians 5:22–23 NLV). When you put those things into action, people will see them and want them too—and the fruit will keep on growing.

Dear God, grow Your fruit of the Spirit in my heart and help me share them with others. Amen.

I'M THE BOSS OF ME

A man who cannot rule his own spirit is like
a city whose walls are broken down.
PROVERBS 25:28 NLV

What if you could do whatever you wanted whenever you wanted? If you didn't want to go to school, you could stay home. You could drink as much soda and eat all the candy, chips, and junk food you wanted. You could stay up all night if you wanted! Wouldn't that be fun? It might be fun for a while, but before long, you wouldn't have learned anything because you weren't in school. You'd be sick from eating all that food, and you'd be tired from getting no sleep. One of the good "fruits" the Holy Spirit puts inside your heart is being the boss of your own desires. When you do what God wants you to do, you keep sin from sneaking into your life. You are the boss of you when it comes to what you allow to grow inside your heart. Grow only good things that come from God.

Dear God, guide me to do what You want me to do instead of what I want to do. Amen.

BOSSY GIRLS

Don't be bossy to those people who are in your care, but set an example for them.

1 PETER 5:3 CEV

You are the sort of girl who is kind, patient, loving, gentle, compassionate, and caring. There are many words to describe your good behavior. You are never bossy, but you know what bossiness looks like. You see other girls being bossy at school. They love telling people what to do. Their way is always right, and everyone else's way of doing things is wrong. They don't allow others to speak or offer ideas. They push ahead, always wanting to be first, and they don't play well or work well on projects with others. Bossy people like to be in control of things all the time. It's never easy being on the receiving end of someone's bossiness, but you will please God when you set a good example. You know how to behave, so let your behavior shine! Show by your own behavior what it means to cooperate, to let others have a turn and have their ideas heard and respected.

Dear God, I will honor You by letting my good behavior shine. Amen.

LET YOUR LIGHT SHINE

You are God's children and no one can talk against you, even in a sin-loving and sin-sick world. You are to shine as lights among the sinful people of this world.
PHILIPPIANS 2:15 NLV

Jesus said that when you do your best to be more like Him, your good behavior shines like a bright, inviting light. You become an example for others of how to behave. Jesus also said that if you had a light in the darkness, you wouldn't hide it under something. Instead, you would let your light shine (Matthew 5:15). He meant that you should never hide your good behavior if it is unpopular or if others make fun of you. When you behave well, you are like a light in the darkness for those who don't know Jesus. You light the way for them to see what good behavior looks like and to want it for themselves. Seeing how you behave might be just what others need to ask Jesus to come into their hearts. So don't hide your light. Let it shine!

Dear Jesus, I will let my good behavior shine like a light, even if others talk against me. Amen.

LEADERSHIP

[A good leader] must like to take people into his home. He must love what is good. He must be able to think well and do all things in the right way. He must live a holy life and be the boss over his own desires.

TITUS 1:8 NLV

Following Jesus and trying to be like Him is good, but Jesus also wants you to be a leader. A leader is someone who welcomes others. You are a leader when you step up and welcome new kids into your life. You are a leader when your good behavior makes others take notice and want to be more like you. A good leader is wise. You are becoming wiser every day. You are learning to make wise decisions, the kinds of decisions that please God. That wisdom will help you lead others in the right direction. Maybe the most difficult part of being a leader is doing what God wants instead of what you want. You're working on that and getting better at it each day. Can you think of other ways to be a good leader?

Dear Jesus, please help me to lead others toward You. Amen.

HOSPITALITY

Offer hospitality to one another without grumbling.
1 Peter 4:9 NIV

Hospitality. What do you think it means? You might recognize the word *hospital* in there, but it has nothing to do with health, hospitals, or doctors. Hospitality is simply welcoming others in a friendly, caring way. If you plan to have visitors to your home, hospitality is preparing for them so they will feel welcome and cared for while they are in your house. Imagine yourself asking a few girlfriends to a sleepover and then doing nothing to prepare. When your guests arrive, you haven't thought of having some of their favorite snacks ready for them or extra pillows and blankets so they'll be comfortable while they sleep. Imagine yourself sleeping in your warm, soft, comfortable bed while they curl up on the cold, hard floor. That wouldn't be hospitality! The Bible says we should offer hospitality willingly. We should treat our guests as we would Jesus if He came to our home. How do you think you would prepare for Jesus if He came for a visit?

Dear God, remind me to offer hospitality to all the visitors who come to my house. Amen.

STRANGERS

Do not forget to show hospitality to strangers, for by so doing some people have shown hospitality to angels without knowing it.

HEBREWS 13:2 NIV

If a stranger rushed in and saved you from drowning or stepping off a curb in front of a bus, you would first thank God, and then you would want to thank that stranger. But what if that person wasn't there anymore and you couldn't find them anywhere? Things like that have happened. You wonder, *Could it have been an angel?* The Bible says that God's angels are everywhere, watching over and helping us (Psalm 91:11–12). Hebrews 13:2 is a reminder to show hospitality not just to people you know but also to strangers. It means you should be kind and treat everyone just as you would an angel if you met one in person. Share Hebrews 13:2 with your parents and talk about the best ways to show kindness to strangers. Think about ways you could welcome new families into your church or your neighborhood.

Dear God, thank You for sending Your angels to watch over and care for me. Amen.

I'M THAT GIRL!

You are now children of God because you have put your trust in Christ Jesus.
GALATIANS 3:26 NLV

Look in the mirror. Who is that girl looking back at you? Yes, you see a girl who is God's unique, special creation. But now you see even more! You see a girl who knows God better because she has been learning more about Him. You see a girl who can be certain that God loves her. He loves her so much that He sent His Son, Jesus, to make a way for her to live forever with Him in heaven someday. You see a girl who knows Jesus and trusts Him as her friend. You see someone who has been finding out what God says is right and wrong and what pleases Him. You see someone who is learning more about prayer and is becoming more comfortable talking with God and listening to His voice inside her heart. Who is that girl? Why, *you* are that girl! His girl! A much-loved child of God.

Dear God, thank You for teaching me more about You. Help me to know You even better. Keep teaching me throughout my life. Amen.

HOLD ON TO YOUR FAITH

Every child of God has power over the sins of the world. The way we have power over the sins of the world is by our faith.

1 JOHN 5:4 NLV

You can't see God, Jesus, or God's angels all around you. But God, His angels, and Jesus are real. The Bible tells you so. All of its words are true. You can believe without seeing because you have faith. That means you know in your heart that everything you've learned about God and Jesus is true. As long as you keep carrying that faith with you, you'll have God's superpower inside your heart. The Bible says you can use that power to overcome the sins of the world. So hold tightly to your faith. Take it with you every day. And if anything gets in your way, use it! Remember who you are—a child of God. Your heavenly Father is with you all the time. He will protect and take care of you.

Dear God, I believe You are real. I know You love me. You are with me always, watching over and protecting me. Thank You for being my heavenly Father. Amen.

SCRIPTURE INDEX

OLD TESTAMENT